Birth
of a Family

Birth
of a Family

LIFE SAVING CONNECTIONS
Stuart Carver and Vickie Carver

For information about this title or to order other books and/or electronic media, contact the publisher:

ReGen Creative, LLC
P.O. Box 157
Gulf Hammock, FL 32639
(813) 388-7819
Email: SCarver@FamilyGodsWay.com

ISBNs:
978-0-9882387-5-6 (hardcover)
978-0-9882387-6-3 (eBook)

Printed in the United States of America

Created by God and dedicated to
His love for life and family.

People Say

"I learned not only to be a good father and husband but also to be a Godly man . . . to lead my household in love and strength, and not in fear. I have been able to share what I've been learning with others close to me, like my brother."

 —ANDREW, a Birth of a Family Participant

"We were scared about being pregnant and were feeling pressure to have an abortion when the ultrasound revealed we had twins. We learned the importance of marriage and how God makes a difference. We both committed our hearts to Christ, are engaged, and plan to get married soon!"

 —BRIAN, a Birth of a Family Participant

"When I first heard about this, I just knew this was not for me. But after the first conversation, I thought, 'Why not try it? It doesn't seem that bad.' As time went on, I actually got into it and was excited about it. It was nothing like what I thought it would be. Before, we were on a downward spiral, and I mean *fast*! It turned everything around. It made me see things in a whole new way."

 —JAMES, a Birth of a Family Participant

"It's wonderful. I've seen differences made in people's lives. It works. If we can help one child to have a mother and father together, it's worth anything. Any amount of money. Any amount of time. Anything."

 —BARB, a Birth of a Family Mentor

"At the beginning, I wasn't really open about religion or God. Now I'm so openly willing to put everything in His hands. I pray almost every night. I have learned that family and relationships matter."

 —RANDAL, a Birth of a Family Participant

"178 couples have been mentored. Many made decisions for Christ, and the future of their families has been significantly impacted."
—KAREN BROOKS, Executive Director, Choices Pregnancy Center, Brandon, Florida

"People's lives and their kids' and their grandkids' lives are being changed for eternity. God is changing hearts."
—PAUL, a Birth of a Family Facilitator

CONTENTS

PREFACE

In 1992, God connected us to life-affirming ministry. Since then, many of our most treasured friendships and many of the most miraculous transformations we have witnessed have occurred while we were serving life ministries around the world.

God gave us two perspectives that sometimes seem at least a little out of the ordinary, even among our cherished life-ministry cohorts.

- ◉ Threats to pre-born lives is first and foremost, a family issue.

- ◉ In God's eyes, life-affirming ministry is not a parachurch ministry.

Chronic problems like threats to pre-born lives, poverty, and adverse childhood experiences cannot be solved without boldly and courageously addressing the root cause. Fathers' hearts turned away from their children and families is the leading root cause of our most troubling problems.

No agency on Earth is more expressly commanded and expertly equipped to address root causes like this than the Body of Christ.

This book is a recipe for making two urgent and challenging connections the way God wants them to be made.

- ◉ Fathers' hearts connected to their families and children

- ◉ The Body of Christ connected to life-affirming ministry

The same recipe shared in this book has been used many times in diverse places around the world. Because creating new Birth of a Family communities correlates so well with preparing a sensational meal, this book is written in the form of a seven-ingredient recipe.

You will see this special recipe from two distinct perspectives. In the first part of this book, CREATED, you will get a deep inside look at how other people and other agencies have used this special recipe to create new Birth of a Family communities in various places around the world. In the second part of this book, CREATING, you will be guided step by step through each of the seven ingredients in this recipe to create your own unique Birth of a Family communities.

GRATITUDE

To say that *Birth of a Family has been wildly popular* would be an overstatement. To say that Birth of a Family has been wildly successful would be true.

God inspired the creation of Birth of a Family through a series of events that cannot be credited to human beings alone. The idea of connecting fathers' hearts to their families and children and connecting the Body of Christ to life-affirming ministry is so ambitious and innovative, only the bold and brave have done it.

Today, the most substantial features of Birth of a Family are the hundreds of real-life stories about unimaginable change. In and of itself, Birth of a Family does not create these stories. People do. Birth of a Family creates the opportunity, but *people make the difference*.

Over the decades, the bold, brave, and often sacrificial participation of hundreds of people and agencies creating new Birth of a Family communities have made it what it is today. This book would have never been written without them. The cooperative teamwork has been extraordinary. To this day, we have never seen anything like it.

FOREWORD

There can be a moment in a man's life when he shifts his posture. Common culture today breeds in men a laid-back commitment to relationships. Distance, emotionally and relationally, protects and preserves the all-important self. But if the truth can sink in—that a man is a father, his eyes both brighten and intensify. As he literally leans in a little closer, Birth of a Family draws him in.

Even amidst the disintegration of the family that our fractured and flawed secular culture is inflicting upon the family, that man's heart turns, and he begins to take on the mantle of godly leadership and biblical responsibility. He moves beyond selfishness to recognize his role with those God has gifted him. As he takes on this role, his partner is supported and able to feel some sense of certainty and security.

That's what Stuart and Vickie have carefully cultivated in Birth of a Family. They call fathers into their biblical roles of providing for and protecting the family they have helped create. And they train others to do the same—especially pregnancy-help ministries who are already engaged with the mom and baby and who are eager to invite new fathers to lean in and step up.

The fruit of their ministry is evident wherever they go. From Florida to Michigan, from Uganda to Timisoara, Romania, they have inspired and engaged ministry to and for young fathers. Families are strengthened. Life decisions are affirmed. Biblical truth is declared. God's Kingdom is made manifest.

The Carvers lean in, even jump in, where they see the opportunity to champion God's way for family. They give their all to make it possible for others to give their all. You'll be blessed to lean in with them as well.

—JOR-EL GODSEY, President, Heartbeat International

INTRODUCTION

Are you looking for better ways to protect pre-born lives and connect the Body of Christ to life-affirming ministry? Are you frustrated by recidivism and cycles of unhealthy relationships? Do you believe children need their fathers? Will it be possible to effectively address our most troubling problems like poverty, abuse, neglect, mental illness, and addiction without completing family circles with fathers?

When fathers' hearts are connected to their children and the Body of Christ is connected to life-affirming ministry like God wants them connected:

- ◉ Demand for abortion goes down

- ◉ Childhood outcomes improve

- ◉ Unhealthy relationships go down

- ◉ Volunteering goes up

- ◉ Poverty, and hunger, addiction, and incarceration go down

- ◉ Families become safer and stronger

- ◉ Stronger families contribute to stronger communities

- ◉ Generational and eternal change happens

Birth of a Family© is a proven relational-discipleship platform that connects fathers' hearts to their children and the Body of Christ to life-affirming ministry the way God wants them to be connected.

In 2006, James was one of the very first fathers to experience Birth of a Family. After participating in Birth of a Family activities with the mother of his child, James made a comment that reminds us why we do this. He said, "Birth of a Family turned everything around. It helped me see things in a whole new way." That's our dream come true.

We have a favorite family recipe for homemade vanilla ice cream that has been handed down over at least five generations. This recipe is hand-written on a worn card stained with vanilla extract. It is a special recipe that is well worth sharing.

> *"Birth of a Family turned everything around. It helped me see things in a whole new way."*

The Birth of a Family recipe is also worth sharing. This book contains a proven special recipe you can use to create your own unique Birth of a Family communities.

Many recipes include a photograph of what the finished product of that recipe can look like. In the first section of this book, CREATED, true stories and case studies are used to give you an authentic look at how this special recipe has been successfully used in a wide range of diverse situations.

In the second section of this book, CREATING, you get to use the recipe yourself. CREATING is a step-by-step guide through the same recipe that has been used for years to create unique Birth of a Family communities.

SUGGESTIONS

⊙ Relax. This book is not intended to persuade you to create new Birth of a Family communities. Only God should do that.

⊙ Dream. Imagine the possibilities of connecting fathers' hearts to their children and connecting the Body of Christ to life-affirming ministry the way God wants them to be connected.

⊙ Create. As you feel led by God, use this proven recipe to create new Birth of a Family communities that are uniquely relevant to you, your situation, and the people being served.

PART ONE

CREATED

Life Saving Connections Made

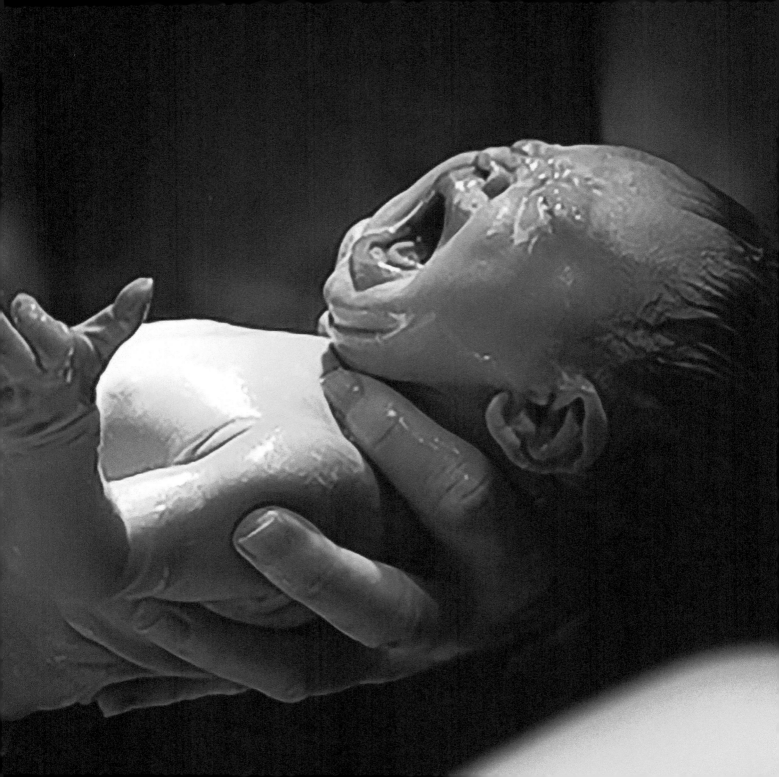

CREATED

"Birth of a Family is innovative, engaging, and transformational. To this day, I've never seen anything like it."
—Birth of a Family Facilitator

In *the first section of this book*, ten true-case studies will give you an inside look at how others have used this special recipe to create new Birth of a Family communities. You will discover how others have:

- ◉ Responded to the compelling drive of God's call to find a better way

- ◉ Scaled and adapted their Birth of a Family communities to many diverse situations and people

- ◉ Increased volunteering by two and three times

- ◉ Remained persistently committed through challenges

- ◉ Experienced the fruit of connecting fathers' hearts to their children and the Body of Christ to life-affirming ministry.

> *"I've never seen anything like it."*

WE CAN

CASE STUDY 1

The first true-case study is a young woman's story about her experiences with Birth of a Family. In her story, you will see how connecting a father's heart to his children and the Body of Christ to life-affirming ministry eliminated the threat of abortion and created a family no one thought was possible.

"Pregnancy was the last thing on my mind. I denied all the clear signs and convinced myself overeating had caused my weight gain.

> "Pregnancy was the last thing on my mind."

My older sister and I shared a bedroom and bathroom. She blew me away one day when she asked if I were pregnant. I denied it at first, but, later that day, I asked her not to tell anyone.

She bought a pregnancy test and left it on our dresser. I took it. No surprise, it came out positive. Still, I didn't comprehend being pregnant. I told my boyfriend. He reacted just like you would expect a seventeen-year-old boy to react and started acting weird afterward. We were both clueless juniors in high school.

My changing body became more difficult to disguise. Each day I felt more alone than the day before. I knew I needed help but was too afraid and too embarrassed to ask. While in the car with my friend Marilyn, I saw a place I'd never noticed before. It was a pregnancy-resource center. It was next door to a dentist's office. I remember thinking, *If my tooth hurt, I would go to that dentist. I'm pregnant! Why not go to that pregnancy-resource center?*

When I told Marilyn I was pregnant, she said she knew. My sister had told her. That afternoon, Marilyn went with me to check out the pregnancy-resource center.

At the pregnancy center, I learned I was further along than I thought. A few weeks later, while sitting in an algebra class, I felt my baby fluttering. It was the first time I'd felt a connection with my baby.

My body really looked pregnant. Everyone knew, and my boyfriend was acting like he couldn't handle this anymore. We each felt very differently about the pregnancy. In his mind, I was the only one who was pregnant.

On a hot summer morning, my mom and I were putting away groceries when I realized I was standing in a puddle of water. She knew right away. That evening, I was nursing my newborn son, Gabriel. My boyfriend was there. He seemed to switch between two personalities—one that adored his son Gabriel and another who wanted to run as far and as fast as he could. We were not getting along, but I tried to remember that he was Gabriel's father.

Our counselor at the pregnancy-resource center also came to the hospital that night to visit with us. Everyone at the center had been so helpful. I don't know how I could have done this without them.

Our counselor had encouraged my boyfriend and me to attend Birth of a Family activities. I liked the idea, but my boyfriend would never commit.

There in the hospital on the night Gabriel was born, just before she left, our counselor suggested Birth of a Family again. The room got quiet except for hospital noises.

After our counselor left the room, my boyfriend and I had our first serious conversation about the future. We were just two kids who were supposed to begin our senior year of high school in two weeks. This wasn't what we thought life would be like. We talked about how unprepared we were.

Then it occurred to us that we were discussing the wrong issues for the wrong reasons. Gabriel was there in our arms, right now. He wasn't just going to wait around for us while we got it together. He was going to grow up, regardless of our feelings about family and parenting.

Until that moment, we had never considered anything but our own selfish agendas. We decided to give Birth of a Family a try.

Three weeks later, my boyfriend, our son, Gabriel, and I went to our first Birth of a Family group meeting at the pregnancy center. There were two other couples, three single moms, and several older couples there. Even though my boyfriend was awkward, we were hooked on Birth of a Family the very first time we went.

We'd both grown up without fathers. Our moms were great, but we had never experienced a family the way it's supposed to be.

By our third meeting with the Birth of a Family group, I hardly recognized the lost boy I had begged to go with me just weeks before. The lights just kept coming on.

> "We were hooked on Birth of a Family the very first time we went."

One of the older couples in the Birth of a Family group took a special interest in us. We later learned they were trained Mentors. They had been married for longer than we had been alive and admitted to having problems and challenges, just like us. It was the first time we had ever gotten an inside look at a family that stayed together.

Everyone usually hung around for a while after the Birth of a Family meetings ended. After the sixth meeting, I turned to ask one of our Mentors to hold Gabriel for a minute. When I turned back toward my boyfriend, he was kneeling near me, reaching for my hand.

Even though I knew exactly what was happening, I could not believe it. I could hardly see my boyfriend through my tears. He asked me to marry him and committed to becoming the best husband and father he could be. He was transforming into just the kind of man I wanted my husband and the father of my children to be. He wasn't perfect. He was just willing to commit to a lifelong relationship with his wife and children and to do all he could do to care for us, no matter what we faced.

We finished high school that year with a newborn toddler. Our friends from Birth of a Family helped us arrange our wedding at their church. We've been married for two years now. Gabriel has a little sister named Lois, and their daddy is home with us.

Even though we do not go to Birth of a Family activities right now, we continue spending time with our Mentors doing fun stuff and going to church. We still need a lot of help. I never imagined I would be able to say this, but we can do this. We can have a family that stays together."

> *"We can have a family that stays together."*

FATHERS' HEARTS TURNED

In Case Study 1, a father's heart turned. Fathers' hearts turned away from their own children is a bewildering phenomenon. It just doesn't make sense that men could be so disconnected from their own children that they'd rather see them die.

In the world we live in today, our expectations for men have sunk so pitifully low that fathers can easily remain disconnected from pregnancy, childbirth, and parenthood without shame or notice. It has become the norm. Birth of a Family creates a new normal.[1]

> *"Birth of a Family creates a new normal."*

When we don't expect much from men, we don't get much from men. In other words, if we do not expect men to be connected to their children, we shouldn't be surprised when they aren't. Birth of a Family raises expectations for fathers.[2]

Research proves that, given time and the right kind of support, the hearts of fathers that may not be turned toward their children at first can be turned toward them. In Case Study 1, Birth of a Family created a window of opportunity where the young father could be exposed to the right kind of support at the right time.

---

1 Lau Clayton C. "The Lives of Young Fathers: A Review of Selected Evidence." *Soc Policy Soc.* 2016 Jan;15(1):129-140. doi: 10.1017/S1474746415000470. PMID: 26740798; PMCID: PMC4697291.

2 Speak, Suzanne, S. J. Cameron, and Rose Gilroy. "Young single fathers: participation in fatherhood—barriers and bridges." Family Policy Studies Centre, 1997

BODY OF CHRIST CONNECTED

Connecting fathers' hearts to their children and the Body of Christ to life-affirming ministry is a 5,000-year-old problem. (Leviticus 20)

"*Shamefully silent and appallingly passive.* These are the words that come to mind when I consider my approach to the issue of abortion for the majority of my life as a Christian and my ministry in the church. Until a few years ago, I barely talked about it. I viewed abortion as a political issue about which I had no need to be personally concerned. I failed to realize that abortion is a biblical issue about which I had great need to be deeply concerned." —David Platt, pastor, author, and former International Mission Board President.[3]

> "*Shamefully silent and appallingly passive.*"

Even regular church attenders experiencing pregnancy as a crisis feel more shame than support from their churches and would not recommend that others experiencing similar circumstances discuss their situations with people at church.[4]

In CASE STUDY 1, Birth of a Family bridged the untenable gap between the Body of Christ and life-affirming ministry. People who may have never interacted otherwise built strong relationships where much needed mentoring and support could happen.

3 *Counter Culture: Following Christ in an Anti-Christian Age*, David Platt, Tyndale House Publishers, Inc
4 Dozier, J. L., Hennink, M., Mosley, E., Narasimhan, S., Pringle, J., Clarke, L., Blevins, J., James-Portis, L., Keithan, R., Hall, K. S., & Rice, W. S. (2020). Abortion attitudes, religious and moral beliefs, and pastoral care among Protestant religious leaders in Georgia. *PloS one*, 15(7), e0235971. https://doi.org/10.1371/journal.pone.0235971

A BETTER
WAY

CASE STUDY 2

Dreams can come true. The next case study is special. It is the story about the very first Birth of a Family community ever created. It happened in 2006, at LifeCare of Brandon in Florida.

The seven key ingredients of this special recipe are revealed in this case study. It all began with a call from God to find a better way.

LifeCare's journey began when their Founder and Executive Director, Laura Jean (Cookie) Gray, became frustrated with the status quo and was inspired by God to get to the root of the problem. Cookie said, "For years, I have watched numbers of young women come into our center dealing with their unplanned pregnancies, almost always alone. I kept thinking, *Something is missing here. Where are the fathers of these babies? We have to find a better way!*"

Since 1993, we have been involved in life-affirming ministry in a variety of capacities. That is how Cookie Gray and Stuart became ministry cohorts and close friends. After twenty years as the executive director of the pregnancy-resource center she founded, Cookie asked Stuart if he would consider writing a Bible-study curriculum that could be used with men and fathers involved with LifeCare's clients. Stuart's answer to Cookie was, "Yes." Seeking Him about how He wanted this Bible study to look, God showed Stuart that He had something far more than a men's Bible study in mind.

> "We have to find
>
> a better way!"

God wanted a relational-discipleship experience that deeply engages the Body of Christ in reaching the root cause of threats to pre-born lives.

Even though it was far more than Cookie asked, our small organization began research and development the very next day. Several weeks later, Stuart met with Cookie. Up to that point, he had only hinted to Cookie how far out of the box he felt God leading.

After sharing the proposal with Cookie, we were all stunned. Cookie wasn't disappointed or overwhelmed. She was elated. God was inspiring Cookie the same way he was inspiring us. The synergy of God's call during those moments was riveting.

Because of its innovative nature, Cookie asked us to put together a formal presentation for LifeCare's staff and Board of Directors to consider. The conference room was full when the proposal was presented. These life-ministry leaders had been operating a very successful pregnancy-resource center for more than two decades.

As expected, initially, there was a hint of skepticism. About halfway through the initial presentation, however, it was like the whole room did a 180-degree turnabout! The nature of the questions being asked shifted from *why* this should be done to *how* we were going to do this. The presentation ended with a courageous and enthusiastically unanimous vote to create the very first Birth of a Family community.

The next step involved developing awareness about LifeCare's unique situation and the people who would be served, using a site survey, a needs survey, and a demographic survey of the surrounding community.

SITE SURVEY HIGHLIGHTS

- LifeCare was located in a quickly growing suburb of Tampa, Florida

- The center was very small, about 1,100 square feet

- Parking was inadequate, even for the regular daily activities

- LifeCare served about 220 client visits a month, had a staff of seven, with about 18 people volunteering at least one hour per week

- LifeCare specialized in providing adoption services but had not yet developed ultrasound capabilities

- Numerous abortion mills were nearby

NEEDS SURVEY HIGHLIGHTS

- Most of the people LifeCare served had never experienced healthy family
- Most clients served had little, if any, support, or the support they had was counterproductive
- Vital services like mental-health counseling were difficult to access
- No relational-discipleship connections with area churches existed

DEMOGRAPHIC SURVEY HIGHLIGHTS

- Most clients lived within a 20-minute drive of the center
- Most female clients were not accompanied by the fathers of their children to visits
- More than one third of clients had been clients of the center before
- Abortion vulnerability was high
- Chronic issues included unhealthy, unsupportive relationships, addiction, abuse, and adverse childhood experiences
- Chronic needs included mental-health counseling, employment, housing, and transportation

The awareness gained through these three surveys was used to develop a plan for creating Birth of a Family communities that were uniquely suited to LifeCare's situation and the people they were serving.

BIRTH OF A FAMILY PLAN HIGHLIGHTS

- ◉ About forty LifeCare clients, partners, friends, and family were expected to participate in Birth of a Family activities each year.

- ◉ About twenty-five people from the Body of Christ would be enlisted, equipped, and engaged as volunteer Coordinators, Facilitators, and Mentors each year.

- ◉ Birth of a Family activities would occur on Tuesday evenings from 6:00 p.m. to 7:30 p.m. in a large classroom provided by a supporting church located near the center.

- ◉ Initially, no childcare was provided. Participants could arrange for their own childcare or bring their young children with them to activities.

People and relationships are the key catalysts in Birth of a Family. People of the Body of Christ were enlisted, equipped, and engaged to serve as volunteer Coordinators, Facilitators, and Mentors. Pregnancy-center clients and co-parents were invited to participate in recurring Birth of a Family relational-discipleship activities. With dates set and new volunteer work commissioned, the table was set for the first-ever Birth of a Family relational-discipleship activities to begin.

LifeCare's new Birth of a Family community came to life on a Tuesday evening. Two Facilitators, four Mentors, and four pregnancy-center clients participated in the first of many Birth of a Family activities to come. These relational-discipleship experiences were unlike anything any of them had ever experienced. Never before had fathers gotten so involved. Never before had people of the Body of Christ built such close, supportive relationships with pregnancy-center clients. The changes were remarkable.

> *"People and relationships are the key catalysts in Birth of a Family."*

Not only did people change, they wanted to *keep* changing. In a March 22, 2007 *Tampa Tribune* article about Birth of a Family, a Mentor said, "We want them to see the light well enough to reach for the rest on their own."[5]

LifeCare's brand-new Birth of a Family community grew quickly and soon included 24 people from the Body of Christ who served as volunteer Coordinators, Facilitators, and Mentors. Relationships developed that continue to this day. After a year of activities, evaluation of LifeCare's Birth of a Family community revealed that the center had more than doubled its number of active volunteers and drawn in more than $26,000 in new financial support. Pregnancy-center clients began getting married and were connected to local churches. Male Participants started a small group for fathers.

Three years later, LifeCare Executive Director Karen Brooks said, "178 couples have been mentored. Many made decisions for Christ, and the future of their families has been significantly impacted by Birth of a Family."

In 2006, when Birth of a Family became the better way she was looking for, Cookie said, "The success of Birth of a Family has been phenomenal. Many people we serve admit that they never had good role models. Some men tell us, 'I do not know how to be a husband or a father.' After more than 20 years of serving as a pregnancy-resource center director, I am now seeing one of my dreams come true. We are reaching the fathers."

> *"I am now seeing one of my dreams come true. We are reaching the fathers."*

---

5 "Coaching Couples," *The Tampa Tribune*, Yvette Hamett, March 22, 2007

RECIPE

A recipe that is consistently successful is like a trusted friend.

Before the next true-case study, reflect on LifeCare's story to see the seven key ingredients of this special recipe in action. They are the same seven key ingredients still in use today.

ABIDING
Becoming frustrated with recidivism and the status quo, Cookie Gray, the Founder and Executive Director of LifeCare, began asking God for a better way. What God revealed was more than she expected. Cookie chose to abide in God's call even though she didn't fully understand it at first.

AWARENESS
Using Site Survey, Needs Surveys, and Demographic Surveys, LifeCare increased their awareness of their unique situation and of the people they would be serving.

PLAN
Awareness empowered relevant planning that mapped out the details for creating their new Birth of a Family communities.

TEAM BUILD
LifeCare's staff didn't just do more work. New people of the Body of Christ, including men and families, were engaged in key volunteer roles as Birth of a Family Coordinators, Facilitators, and Mentors.

DILIGENCE
Even though no one had ever done this before, our work was done well and persistently, resulting in connecting fathers' hearts to their children and the Body of Christ to life-affirming ministry the way God wants them to be connected.

OPTIMIZE

Like most life-affirming ministries, LifeCare was very busy. Initially, more activity was a challenge for them to integrate. Looking back, it became obvious that, by creating their Birth of a Family community, LifeCare was able not only to get more done but also to do it better.

EVALUATION

By the fruit, it shall be known. Did Birth of a Family work for LifeCare? The facts speak for themselves.

AT LIFECARE:

- ◉ Fathers' hearts turned

- ◉ The Body of Christ connected like they never had before

- ◉ Volunteering doubled in fifteen months

- ◉ Abortion risk was reduced

- ◉ Pregnancy-center clients were married

- ◉ Children had present fathers

- ◉ Mothers had support

- ◉ New in-kind and cash support was generated

> *The facts speak for themselves.*

This recipe for creating new Birth of a Family communities has stood the test of time. To this day, it includes the same seven key ingredients. The remaining true-case studies will demonstrate each of these seven key ingredients in order while giving you an inside look at some of the diverse opportunities, difficult challenges, and surprising victories that have been experienced.

ABIDING

CASE STUDY 3

Birth
of a Family
RECIPE

INGREDIENT:

ABIDING

When it is God's idea, the results are phenomenal.

OBJECTIVE:

Discover whose idea creating new Birth of a Family communities is.

Our abiding in God's call is like an RSVP for a banquet. *Répondez s'il vous plaît* translates to "Respond, please."

Knowing that you are following God's lead helps when challenges arise. (Isaiah 41:10)

This case study is about a pregnancy center about 40 miles away from LifeCare. Challenges arose right away. This pregnancy center was serving about 100 client visits per month at the time. The director heard about Birth of a Family at LifeCare and felt inspired by God to create their own new Birth of a Family community.

Shortly after the pregnancy-center's director decided to create a new Birth of a Family community, God moved them to a new position in another city. The new executive director needed some time to settle in. Then, they needed to experience God's call to create a new Birth of a Family community at the center. God's call was confirmed.

When the new director presented the plan for Birth of a Family at a board meeting, some on the Board had reasonable fiscal concerns. Although perplexed, the director felt sure God wanted this and wisely waited on the Lord to convince others. The director didn't have to wait for long. Days later, a representative from a local charitable foundation dropped off a check for the full amount needed to fund the creation of their new Birth of a Family community.

That wasn't the last challenge they faced. Being in the Bible Belt, the site survey indicated a large number of churches in the area. Twenty-one churches were invited to help their people of the Body of Christ get involved. The first twenty said, "No." Fortunately, the twenty-first pastor and church said, "Yes." It was an ideal partnership clearly ordained by God.

Another challenge was the small size of the meeting room at the center for Birth of a Family activities. It was so small and the crowds so big that the Facilitators sometimes stood in the hall and guided conversations through the doorway. What could have been a distraction became a humorous reminder to abide through the challenges.

One of the surprising victories in this Birth of a Family community was a high-school couple. They had conceived a child together while still in high school and had already committed to becoming a family for life. Because of their own family histories, however, they needed help learning how to establish a lasting family.

> *"It was an ideal partnership clearly ordained by God."*

After participating for some time, several of the Mentors let the group know they'd need to leave Birth of a Family activities early for the next several weeks to practice for a church play.

The young high-school couple spontaneously asked, "Can we come to see your play?" Surprised and delighted, the Mentors said, "Yes" and arranged transportation for them. The couple and their little baby girl experienced the Gospel at this church, and both the father and mother were baptized there.

Overcoming challenges to God's call was a theme in the making of this case study. Challenges included unexpected leadership changes, fiscal concerns, disinterested churches, and small meeting spaces. The drive to abide God's calling overcame the challenges.

From time to time you will encounter a reminder that this book is not intended to persuade the disinterested. It is meant to guide the driven. Not only has the recipe for creating new Birth of a Family communities stood the test of time, it has stood the test of challenge.

There will be challenges. Even the best recipes can't eliminate challenges. How we respond when challenged is the game changer. In this case study, a small group of tenaciously driven people simply would not allow challenge to deter them. The story doesn't end there though. Their tenacious response to challenge became a transferable habit.

> *"Their tenacious response to challenge became a transferable habit."*

About five years after creating their new Birth of a Family community it was time for a new volunteer team from a new church to take over. When they did, the precedent about dealing with challenge was already set. The new team simply carried on the tradition of facing challenge tenaciously that was handed down from the previous team of Birth of a Family volunteers.

AWARENESS

The best recipes adapt to fresh ingredients that are in season.

A key ingredient in the Birth of a Family recipe is becoming aware of each individual opportunity and of the people being served.

Three surveys are included in this special recipe to assist in developing awareness.

- Site surveys identify unique operational characteristics of agencies and individuals that are creating new Birth of a Family communities

- Needs surveys identify locally unique needs

- Demographic surveys identify the unique characteristics of the people who will be served by new Birth of a Family communities

These surveys have long been helpful in creating unique, relevant and effective Birth of a Family communities.

First Life is a large pregnancy center situated on a megachurch campus in Orlando, Florida. In 2012, when Birth of a Family started at First Life, the center was brand new, spacious, and exquisitely furnished.

Birth
of a Family
RECIPE

INGREDIENT:

AWARENESS

Great cooking favors prepared hands.

OBJECTIVE:

Develop deeper awareness about your situation and the people served.

They had a full complement of talented staff and were serving more than 500 client visits per month. The meeting room at the center in which recurring Birth of a Family relational-discipleship activities occurred easily accommodated more than 70 people and was often full.

When the initial site, needs, and demographic surveys came in, we got a big surprise. First Life was experiencing a large increase in the number of Haitian clients they were serving. Without these initial surveys, we would have missed the opportunity to adapt Birth of a Family to these unique people during that time.

Awareness can also happen spontaneously. In Michigan, a woman who had lost both legs to amputation was participating in Birth of a Family activities. Weeks went by. Relationships developed, and finally, someone noticed that she transported herself to and from activities along the streets and sidewalks in her wheelchair. Weeks more went by, seasons changed, and this Birth of a Family community became more aware of the challenges she faced transporting herself to and from activities through the snow.

Then, the group got to know her enough to become aware of another difficulty. She had no ramp where she lived. In order to navigate the steps in and out of her house, she would get out of her wheelchair, sit down on the porch, push her wheelchair down the steps, move herself down the steps, get back in her wheelchair, and carry on. That's when this community did what Birth of a Family communities do so well. They took it upon themselves to help. About 30 people did what no one else had done. They cleaned up the yard, repaired the porch, and installed a beautiful new aluminum ramp and railing.

This kind of action is common in Birth of a Family communities.

> *"This kind of action is common in Birth of a Family communities."*

As time went on, a shift occurred. These and other kinds of responses became so common that they continued whether Birth of a Family activities were happening or not. Various groups of Birth of a Family volunteers and Participants began helping each other and helping others more and more. They had backyard and lakeside park fellowships, worship and baptisms. People helped people get jobs, houses and cars.

Some might wonder why all this wasn't happening before. Birth of a Family has a predictably consistent way of increasing the awareness of people of the Body of Christ about needs around them. Before Birth of a Family, many of the people involved never interacted with each other. Birth of a Family became the bridge between them.

Once they became aware of each other, the connections developed, relational-discipleship happened and lives changed.

Birth of a Family bridges the untenable gap between the Body of Christ and people served by life-affirming ministries.

The command at the end of Matthew 28 says, "Go." Birth of a Family gives people of the Body of Christ a place to go and roles to play where they can be the hands, feet and hearts of Christ.

PLAN

Great cooking favors prepared hands.

Connecting fathers' hearts to their children and the Body of Christ to life-affirming ministry the way God wants them to be connected is not a casual pursuit. Careful planning makes it possible to scale and adapt the Birth of a Family recipe to virtually any situation, anywhere in the world.

CASE STUDY 5

PLAN TO SCALE

Between 2015 and 2017, Birth of a Family was scaled up to serve the countries of:

- ⊚ Romania (slightly smaller than the U.S. state of Oregon)

- ⊚ Serbia (slightly smaller than the U.S. state of South Carolina)

Appropriate planning made it possible to engage more than 700 people in international collaboration to create Birth of a Family communities in Romania and Serbia.

Birth **of a Family** RECIPE

INGREDIENT:

PLAN

Noble people make noble plans and on those plans they stand.

OBJECTIVE:

Create a Birth of a Family Plan that is uniquely relevant to your situation and the people you will serve.

Abiding God's call began in August 2015, when Ionel Tutac, a Romanian pastor, became familiar with a Birth of a Family community in Atlanta, Georgia. Pastor Tutac felt compelled to get the Body of Christ involved in protecting pre-born lives and improving child outcomes. God inspired him to bring Birth of a Family to Romania and Serbia.

Later that same year, Pastor Tutac and other Romanian cohorts, including a government official, visited Family God's Way in the U.S. to learn more and to start developing their plan to create new Birth of a Family communities in Romania. By mid-2016, a plan and a Romanian NGO (like a nonprofit in the U.S.) had been created for this purpose.

> *"Even though the scale was large, the strategy was simple."*

Even though the scale was large, the strategy was simple. Empower individuals, churches, pastors, and other agencies in Romania and Serbia to create locally relevant Birth of a Family communities.

By January 2016, a team of Romanian nationals were working collaboratively with a U.S. team to translate Birth of a Family resources into the Romanian language. Seven months later, the first 70 sets of Romanian Birth of a Family resources were printed in Romania.

In July 2016, Grace Church in Lugoj, Romania, provided facilities, meals, and transportation for an international team to use as a base of operations while serving in Romania and Serbia. Grace Church also hosted a number of Birth of a Family Informational Workshops, attended by more than 130 pastors and church leaders, 8 government officials, and many people of the Body of Christ. The campaign was also covered by one television station and 10 radio stations.

CASE STUDY 6

PLAN TO ADAPT

In 2011, while speaking at a life-affirming ministry conference in Columbus, Ohio, Stuart met Veronica Nakyewe, the Founder and Director of Comforter's Center in Kampala, Uganda. At that time, Comforter's Center was the only pregnancy-resource center serving this densely populated metropolis of more than two million people.

We are accustomed to meeting American life-affirming ministry cohorts at U.S. conferences. Meeting someone like Veronica from Uganda was unexpected.

Having arrived at the conference center before check-in, people had not yet begun pouring into the large conference center. Far across a very large and virtually empty room, Stuart saw a woman in a wheelchair who looked somewhat disoriented. Carefully approaching, kneeling down to be on eye level, Stuart asked if he could assist. Veronica's first words were, "I was praying the Lord would send someone to me."

Veronica had traveled to the conference center via cab from the airport, where she had just completed the 22-hour plane trip from Entebbe, Uganda, to Columbus, Ohio. The wheelchair in which she sat was borrowed from the conference center. She had traveled to the U.S. alone to learn more about life-affirming ministry.

Having only one workshop presentation to present, the rest of Stuart's time at the conference was open, so Stuart offered to assist Veronica by pushing her wheelchair around the expansive conference center. Over the next two days, a lifelong friendship was forged.

Veronica attended Stuart's workshop. After learning more about Birth of a Family, she asked, "Can we do this in Uganda?" She had been searching for a way to help the single mothers break free from unhealthy relationships and learn how to develop lasting family relationships. After discussing it further, we agreed. We could bring Birth of a Family to Uganda.

> *"Can we do this in Uganda?"*

In 2012, Veronica returned to the U.S., where she spent a number of days with us developing Comforter's Center's plan. Veronica felt led by God to use Birth of a Family in two distinctly different communities:

- ◉ In the densely populated urban community of Kampala

- ◉ In remote villages such as those around the southeastern edges of Lake Kyoga

The opportunity in Uganda was extraordinary. We had never planned to create Birth of a Family in two more distinctly different populations before. In the urban community of Kampala, most Participants lived in the nearby slums, some of the world's largest. In the remote communities, Participants were widely dispersed and traveled almost everywhere on foot.

Never before had we planned for new Birth of a Family communities in a country where abortion was illegal. Despite being illegal in Uganda, abortion was rampant. Many people served by Comforter's Center had experienced abortion multiple times. Unlike the U.S., where abortion has been made safer for mothers, abortion in Uganda can be as dangerous for mothers as it is for pre-born children.

Never before had we developed a Plan to create new Birth of a Family communities in places where husbands could legally have more than one wife. In this culture, secondary wives were treated differently than primary wives. When secondary wives became pregnant, they were frequently abandoned by both their husbands and their churches.

Never had we planned to create new Birth of a Family communities where poverty was so desperately acute. Even the most basic essentials were scarce or nonexistent. Few of the people served had access to clean water, adequate nutrition, reasonable shelter, jobs, sanitation, or transportation.

Broad adaptations from typical Western approaches were required. In the dense, urban community of Kampala, Birth of a Family activities occurred periodically at the center with individuals and small groups. Virtually all Participants were severely impoverished single mothers with little or no support from the fathers of their children. Many lived in the nearby slums, and most were vulnerable to and had experienced multiple previous abortions.

In the remote satellite locations, daylong relational-discipleship activities occurred in small tin churches and under tattered burlap tents. Men, women, and children walked, sometimes long distances, to participate. At one such gathering, the leader of the church hosting the meeting said, "We didn't think you'd come. No one ever comes all the way out here to help us, even when they say they will."

In both of these distinctly unique communities, two problems stood out:

> *"Never before had we planned for new Birth of a Family communities in a country where abortion was illegal."*

- ◉ Hearts of fathers were disconnected from their children

- ◉ The Body of Christ was disconnected from life-affirming ministry

TEAM BUILD

CASE STUDY 7

Team building is to Birth of a Family what good ingredients are to great recipes. With good ingredients, it's hard to go very wrong.

People and relationships are good ingredients. When people of the Body of Christ connect to life-affirming ministry the way God wants them to connect, it's hard to go very wrong.

Birth of a Family communities create a new type of teamwork, in which people of the Body of Christ connect like never before with life-affirming ministry. Birth of a Family teams have often increased the number of active volunteers by two times or more, with many of those new volunteers being men and families.

This case study is about Birth of a Family master team builder Barb Hernandez. Barb learned the importance of building new Birth of a Family teams while serving as a Client Services Director for Westshore Pregnancy and Family Support in Ludington, Michigan.

Barb's Birth of a Family story began when she attended three workshops we provided at a Life Matters Worldwide conference in Michigan. During the first workshop, Barb was skeptical. By the second workshop, she was curious. By the third workshop, Barb said, "This is the missing piece!"

Birth
of a Family
RECIPE

INGREDIENT:

TEAM BUILD

With good ingredients, it's hard to go very wrong.

OBJECTIVE:

Engage people in sufficient scale to accomplish your goals and God's desire.

As Barb returned to her work at the pregnancy center with a call to create new Birth of a Family communities, her biggest concern was whether people of the Body of Christ and pregnancy-center clients would participate.

In May 2017, the site survey for the pregnancy center where Barb worked identified 27 churches that supported the center financially. Instead of just inviting one church at a time, Barb created a Birth of a Family social-media group that she used to invite the entire community of people from the Body of Christ to attend her Birth of a Family Informational Workshops. This innovation led to one of the most diverse outpourings of people from the Body of Christ into Birth of a Family relational-discipleship roles ever experienced.

Remarkably, new volunteers included as many men as women. The new volunteers more than tripled the number of active volunteers for the pregnancy center. Most of Barb's new volunteers were men and couples.

Immediately following the 12-week pilot series of Birth of a Family activities, an evaluation was done. In summary, every initial expectation was exceeded, some by far. Outcomes were so surprisingly good that this pilot series of activities was featured in a *Pregnancy Help News* article written by Karen Ingle[6] and featured in the local Ludington *Daily News*.[7]

After the successful pilot group, things changed. No longer was this a mysterious new effort shrouded with skepticism. People of the Body of Christ and clients from the pregnancy center showed up. They were nice to each other, and relational-discipleship became spontaneously effective. Nothing like this had ever happened before. The experience changed not only the community—it changed Barb.

> *"No longer was this a mysterious new effort shrouded with skepticism."*

The new Birth of a Family community grew into other nearby communities, including a community for Spanish-speaking people. In May 2019, the first Spanish-speaking Birth of a Family community (*Nacimiento de una Familia*) celebrated the graduation of their first round of Participants.

In 2020, when everything else was shutting down in one of the toughest states in the U.S. on social gatherings, Birth of a Family activities in Michigan continued. Restricted from meeting in person, they

6 https://pregnancyhelpnews.com/birth-of-a-family-12-week-program-inspires-positive-change-among-michigan-families
7 https://www.shorelinemedia.net/ludington_daily_news/new-program-connects-families/article_c7e6e7a0-f6e8-11e7-87fe-7fb46b40d788.html

met online. The community actually grew stronger. Participants were baptized. Marriages were restored. They did fun things together, like backyard fellowships and community-service projects. They solved tough problems together, like helping families and single mothers get jobs,

> *"Strangers became a caring, connected community."*

achieve sustainable housing, and find reliable cars. Strangers became a caring, connected community.

Barb voluntarily did the work of coordinating all these Birth of a Family activities while still employed as a Client Services Director for the pregnancy center. Eventually, she had to choose. Doing it all was no longer an option. She resigned from her position at the pregnancy center and has since specialized in helping other people and agencies create their own new Birth of a Family communities.

DILIGENCE

Diligence is persistent work carefully done.

This true-case study is about an overall evaluation that occurred when Birth of a Family was about 10 years old. In that 2017 evaluation, we wanted to learn more about why some new Birth of a Family communities appeared to become more sustainable than others. The recipe was sound, but the results varied. We learned three valuable lessons from this 2017 evaluation of Birth of a Family.

The first lesson learned was a lesson we already knew. Our 2017 evaluation confirmed that connecting fathers' hearts to their children and the Body of Christ to life-affirming ministry are ambitious goals.

The second lesson we learned is perplexing. We learned that connecting fathers' hearts to their children and the Body of Christ to life-affirming ministry is not as popular as we thought it would be. In our initial naiveté, we thought all churches and pregnancy centers would love it. Ten years in, we came to grips with the hard fact that this wasn't going to be as popular as we thought it would be.

Birth of a Family
RECIPE

INGREDIENT:

DILIGENCE

Diligence is persistent work carefully done.

OBJECTIVE:

Stimulate a culture of diligence by setting dates and commissioning work.

The third lesson we learned was the clincher. Because connecting fathers' hearts to their children and the Body of Christ to life-affirming ministry is challenging and unpopular, diligent commitment to the persistent work that must be done carefully is essential.

By the time our 2017 study was wrapping up, we'd come to realize that creating new Birth of a Family communities was not going to be wildly popular, just miraculously successful. The study not only confirmed the effectiveness of Birth of a Family, it highlighted the necessity of persistent work carefully done.

From the pregnancy centers and churches involved in the 2017 study until this day, those who chose to create new Birth of a Family tend to have one common characteristic. Desire. They want to see fathers' hearts turned and the Body of Christ connected to life-affirming ministry. It is a peculiar desire that can only be satisfied when the advent of parenthood includes the birth of families where fathers, mothers and children all live, grow and play together in one home.

Unless driven, the persistent work, carefully done, can be difficult to maintain. That is why this book is not intended to persuade the disinterested. It is meant to guide the driven.

Where does this peculiar drive come from? God. After decades of inviting thousands of pregnancy centers and churches to consider creating new Birth of a Family communities, we've learned that it must begin with a piercing call from God to connect fathers' hearts to their children and families and to connect the Body of Christ to life-affirming ministry the way God wants them to be connected.

In a significant way, this peculiar drive to persistently do the work that must be done carefully is a gift from God. That is why this special recipe begins with seeking first, God. While we wish more pregnancy centers and churches would create Birth of a Family communities, until God's gift of this piercing drive occurs, it might be best to wait for it. Or, if you dare, ask for it.

"If you dare, ask for it."

Finally, we have learned over and over again that Satan desperately does not want this done and will oppose the creation of Birth of a Family communities. Amidst opposition, doubts and temptations to give up can creep in.

One of Satan's predictable favorites is discouraging people from participating in regular Birth of a Family activities. When the numbers of people participating is not as high as desired, it is important to remember the value of one life changed. Even when just two or more are gathered for the purpose of turning toward God and His ways, life changing connections happen.

In Case Study 3, the people creating a new Birth of a Family community faced this challenge. Occasionally, there were fewer people participating than they hoped. Nevertheless, they relentlessly pressed on. Their persistent work carefully done resulted in a tradition of diligence that pressed through Satan's opposition and miraculous changes happened.

"Diligence is persistent work carefully done."

OPTIMIZE

Optimization is planned excellence.

Intentional optimization is a distinctive feature of Birth of a Family that empowers the continued pursuit of excellence. Optimization is not a single action. It is an ongoing attitude.

A new Birth of a Family community was created in an urban location where many of the people being served experienced poverty and homelessness. A nearby area was even called "Suitcase City" because of its transient population. Crime was bad, unemployment was high, and needed services were difficult to access.

An early optimization became necessary. Participants would need help getting transportation to and from recurring Birth of a Family activities.

> *"Optimization is not a single action. It is an ongoing attitude."*

A nearby church had a large parking lot that was used during the business week as a mass-transit hub, where people would transfer from city buses to other buses or to their personal vehicles. This Birth of a Family community negotiated an agreement with the church to host Birth of Family activities at that church on Wednesday

Birth of a Family RECIPE

INGREDIENT:

OPTIMIZE

Optimization is planned excellence.

OBJECTIVE:

Optimize Birth of a Family to be especially effective in your situation and with the people being served.

evenings, when church activities were already occurring. Participants could then use public transportation to get to and from Birth of a Family activities. Public-transit vouchers were even provided.

This was not only a creative optimization to a significant problem, it became an *attitude* that opened the door for more surprising breakthroughs no one anticipated.

After Birth of a Family activities had been taking place for a while at the new church location, a Participant couple with two children wanted to get married, but they didn't have the money to pay for wedding expenses.

Because this Birth of a Family community had already wisely optimized by obtaining approval from the State of Florida to use their Birth of a Family activities as a premarital course, Participants were eligible for a 50% discount from the state on their marriage licenses.

Then, the hosting church optimized up another level by offering free access to church facilities for Birth of a Family Participant weddings. The Birth of a Family community helped out with decorations, wedding dresses, and reception food. A number of couples had beautiful weddings that would have otherwise been impossible.

The next optimization came when the hosting church began referring its own church members to use Birth of a Family for their premarital counseling.

The next level-up came when the hosting church opened their baptistry for Participants during church worship services.

Over time, arrangements were made in which regular church childcare was offered to Birth of a Family Participants. The church began providing meals and supporting the group financially.

It would have been difficult to predict in the beginning all of the surprising breakthroughs that an attitude of optimization would empower. Ultimately, this church did more than just let the Birth of a Family community use one of their empty rooms. They connected to life-affirming ministry the way God wants the Body of Christ to connect.

Optimization is planned excellence. As you creatively plan adaptations to Birth of a Family communities to be more relevant to your situation and the people being served, you will increase the excellence of the experiences for everyone involved. Your optimizations will empower you to meet unmet needs, overcome stubborn problems and breakthrough barriers to success.

Optimize

Birth of a Family is designed to adapt. No two situations are exactly alike. Adaptations and optimization are not only helpful, they are needed. Common adaptations have included:

- Offering Birth of a Family activities in other languages

- Providing Birth of a Family activities in more than one place and more than one time

- Including social and community involvement activities

- Creating social media groups for Birth of a Family

- Using other content for Birth of a Family relational discipleship activities

- Improving access to needed services such as mental health counseling

"Optimization is planned excellence."

EVALUATION

Birth of a Family sets the table for generational change.

Evaluation completes the circle. Because we began by seeking God first and abiding by His will, we have the promise of eternal fruit that we can evaluate. Unlike mere human endeavors, with abiding by God's will, miraculous transformation can be expected, validated, and celebrated. (John 15:5) Evaluation is a key part of the Birth of a Family recipe that glorifies God and encourages us.

This case study is about a four-year (2007–2011) evaluation of Birth of a Family. Involved in that study were:

> *"Birth of a Family sets the table for generational change."*

⊙ Seven pregnancy-resource centers that created new Birth of a Family communities

⊙ Twenty-seven churches that supported these new Birth of a Family communities by hosting workshops and activities, providing childcare, food, and transportation, and by encouraging people of the Body of Christ to volunteer

Birth of a Family RECIPE

INGREDIENT:

EVALUATION

Taste and see that Yahweh is good.

OBJECTIVE:

Experience Birth of a Family firsthand. Encounter the fruit. Tell the story.

- Numerous donors, businesses, and charitable foundations

- More than a hundred enlisted, equipped, and engaged Birth of a Family Coordinators, Facilitators, and Mentors

- More than a hundred Participants from pregnancy-resource centers, family, friends, and referrals from churches, family courts, and other ministries.

Does it work? Even though we had already seen it work, we wanted to document how often Birth of a Family experiences turn people toward God and His ways.

In the 2007-2011 study, Participants were asked to complete two surveys. They completed one when they began participating and another after they had participated in at least seven activities. Both surveys were similar allowing differences in responses to measure a change in perspective.

Fifty-two percent (52%) of Participants surveyed indicated their Birth of a Family experiences turned them toward God and His ways!

Why does it work? During the study, survey responses and personal interviews repeatedly indicated that the role modeling, mentoring, and support were the most influential parts of their Birth of a Family experiences.

> *"When connected the way God wants them to be connected, the Body of Christ and life-affirming ministry can be a stunning combination."*

Since the study, we've been able to answer a third and vital question, "Does it last?" Three findings suggest it does.

- First, many of the discipling relationships that begin during Birth of a Family activities continue for many years afterward.

- Second, Biblical covenant weddings among Birth of a Family Participants are not uncommon.

- Finally, once connected the way God wants them to be connected, the Body of Christ and life-affirming ministry tend to remain more connected.

It truly is a stunning combination. Think about it. On one hand, no other agency on Earth is more equipped or more emphatically mandated to engage in relational-discipleship than the Body of Christ. The Body of Christ is expressly called and equipped by God to be the preeminent agent of change in protecting pre-born lives.

On the other hand, no agency on Earth has developed more trust and rapport with people experiencing the advent of parenthood as a crisis than life-affirming ministries. Life-affirming ministries open the door to the Body of Christ so that what neither can achieve apart can be miraculously accomplished together.

> *"When this stunning combination occurs, miraculous transformation can be expected, evaluated and celebrated."*

Birth of a Family creates the bridge between the Body of Christ and life-affirming ministry. When this stunning combination occurs, miraculous transformation can be expected, evaluated and celebrated.

PART TWO

CREATING

Making Life Saving Connections

CREATING

The purpose of the first section of this book, CREATED, was to help you see what Birth of a Family is like through the eyes and hearts of people who have experienced it. Dating back to 2006, when the first new Birth of a Family community was created, you got an inside look at some of the diverse opportunities, difficult challenges, and surprising victories.

The purpose of the second section of this book, CREATING, is to help you create new Birth of a Family communities of your own.

RECIPE

RECIPE

*Y*our relationship with this book is about to change. Instead of hearing how others have experienced Birth of a Family, you are going to be guided step by step through the same special recipe they used to create your own, new Birth of a Family communities.

The CREATING section of this book will follow the same order of seven key ingredients you discovered in the first section of this book, CREATED.

1.	Abiding	John 15
2.	Awareness	Proverbs 4:7
3.	Plan	Isaiah 32:8
4.	Team Build	1 Corinthians 12:12
5.	Diligence	Romans 12:8
6.	Optimize	James 2:14-26
7.	Evaluation	Matthew 7:20

For each of these seven key ingredients, a brief explanation will be followed by a clear objective. Tips will be shared based on best practices over the years. Step-by-step suggestions will be made to help you achieve the objective for each ingredient. Following the step-by-step suggestions, examples will be shared to demonstrate how each ingredient in this special recipe can be creatively scaled and adapted to your unique situation and the people who will be served.

TEMPLATES

This book comes with a huge, innovative advantage: a package of digital templates that are synchronized with this special recipe. These digital templates will give you a substantial head start in creating your own Birth of a Family resources. Not only will these templates save you time, they will provide you with a cohesive, logical planning framework that has worked well for years.

This digital package of templates is available on the Birth of a Family website. Templates are compatible with Microsoft applications such as Word, Excel, and PowerPoint, Apple Pages, Numbers, Keynote and Google Docs, Sheets, and Slides.

BirthofaFamily.org/downloads

Visit the website now. Download the template package, and save it to your digital devices. Then, as you continue reading, follow the recipe in this book, and use these valuable templates to create your own Birth of a Family resources that are adapted to your unique situation and the people who will be served.

Birth of a Family communities are not cut like cookies. Each one is unique.

With this recipe and your free digital templates in hand, you are ready to begin. From this point forward, this recipe is about you, your situation and the unique people that will be involved.

In this second part of this book, CREATING, the recipe will follow the same sequence as in the first part, CREATED. The sequence of this recipe is intentional. Each part of the recipe builds upon the previous part. This recipe is proven in a wide range of circumstances. Every part of this recipe is vital. Nothing should be left out and no substitutions should be made. Take your time and follow the recipe step by step.

"Birth of a Family communities are not cut like cookies. Each one is unique."

The recipe begins with seeking God first. When Birth of a Family communities are God's idea, the results are phenomenal. In the first ingredient of this recipe you will be guided to seek God, hear from Him and share what you believe His will is regarding the creation of new Birth of a Family communities.

Recipe

The Abiding ingredient in this recipe culminates with a written testimony about your experiences with God about this special calling. Throughout the remainder of this recipe, let your experiences with God about this special calling flavor everything else you do.

ABIDING

Ingredient 1

ABIDING

When it is God's idea, the results are phenomenal.

Connecting fathers' hearts to their children and the Body of Christ to life-affirming ministry is a 5,000-year-old problem. If you are curious and brave, read through Leviticus 20. This book is not about persuading you to create new Birth of a Family communities. It is about helping you abide God's will if that's what you believe God wants you to do.

Birth of a Family is effective. The recipe is proven. However, the most important ingredient in this recipe is abiding by the will and call of God. When—not *if*—challenges arise, you need to know that you are doing this because you believe God wants you to.

Seeking God first and abiding by His will and call is emphasized. Connecting fathers' hearts to their children and families and connecting the Body of Christ to life-affirming ministry is colossal kingdom work. God must be in it.

The kinds of changes that happen through Birth of a Family are far more than just mediocre attitude adjustments. They are life changing and life saving.

Birth
of a Family
RECIPE

INGREDIENT:

ABIDING

When it is God's idea, the results are phenomenal.

OBJECTIVE:

Discover whose idea creating new Birth of a Family communities is.

Because creating new Birth of a Family communities is ambitious and the objectives require acts of God to regenerate people and save lives, it is imperative to know that this is something God wants you to do.

Knowing God wants you to create new Birth of a Family communities may give you fresh hope and greater expectations. It will certainly inspire commitment to the diligent and persistent work that must be carefully done. Knowing God wants you to do this may result in camaraderie with God like you have never experienced before.

OBJECTIVE

Discover whose idea creating new Birth of a Family communities is.

TIPS

◉ Be still. Give yourself time to focus on seeking God first. (Matthew 6:33)

◉ Be quiet. Listen for God's still, small voice. (John 10:27)

◉ Be courageous. Boldly follow God's inspiration. (Joshua 1:6-9)

SUGGESTIONS

◉ Even if you already believe God wants you to create new Birth of a Family communities, seek His affirmation once more, please. (Matthew 7:7-8)

◉ Listen for God's responses. (2 Peter 1:20-21)

◉ In prayer between just you and God, in a spirit of stillness, simply ask God the question, "Is this what you want me to do?" Then quietly wait. Avoid reasoning. It isn't necessary. Just wait and see what God will reveal to you.

◉ Consider inviting someone else to join you in seeking God about this question. (Matthew 18:20)

◉ Seek Him until you can answer this question: "Whose idea is this?" (Matthew 6:10)

- ◉ Get in step with God. (John 15:4)

- ◉ When you believe God wants you to create new Birth of a Family communities, with resolute assurance, set your face like flint toward abiding this spectacular call. (Isaiah 50:7)

- ◉ As you abide, do so boldly and courageously. (Joshua 1:9)

- ◉ Celebrate as you proceed. God is glorified as fruit is born out of our abiding. Abiding God's will and call is one of the richest forms of worship that can occur between God and His people. (John 15:7-11)

- ◉ Write a statement about your call to create new Birth of a Family communities. Your statement can acknowledge God, cast vision for yourself and others, and may inspire you to think bigger while using this recipe.

EXAMPLE

"Burdened by threats to pre-born lives, the state of fatherhood and the disconnect between the Body of Christ and life-affirming ministry, I sought God. I believe God wants me to play a role in creating new Birth of a Family communities."

"Abiding God's will and call is one of the richest forms of worship that can occur between God and His people."

There may be no other place in this recipe where your words are more crucial. Creating new Birth of a Family communities must be inspired by God. Seek first God. If God is inspiring you, your statement will similarly inspire others who will join you in this journey.

AWARENESS

Ingredient 2

AWARENESS

God encourages us to get understanding.
—Proverbs 2:2-5

Great cooking favors prepared hands.

Awareness is the second key ingredient in the Birth of a Family recipe. Developing deeper awareness empowers you to create new Birth of a Family communities that are relevant to any situation and to any people, anywhere in the world.

OBJECTIVE

Develop deeper awareness about your situation and the people who will be served.

SOMETHING NEW

At this point in the recipe, you will start something new. You will begin using templates in a package available for download from the Birth of a Family website. This template package gives you a big head start in creating your own Birth of a Family resources. Templates are synchronized with the seven ingredients in this book. As you proceed with this recipe, the appropriate templates will

---

INGREDIENT:

AWARENESS

Great cooking favors prepared hands.

OBJECTIVE:
Develop deeper awareness about your situation and the people served.

be suggested. Open the suggested templates, and use them to create your own Birth of a Family resources that are adapted to your unique situation and the people who will be served.

Visit the website now. Download the template package. Before using them, consider saving the entire package of unedited templates so that they can be easily accessed and used. Saving the unedited templates will also help if you need a fresh start or to use them again to create more Birth of a Family communities.

GET STARTED

SURVEYS

Developing deeper awareness about your situation and the people who will be served is accomplished using three surveys. The three surveys are:

- **Site Survey**
  Like fingerprints, no two opportunities to create Birth of a Family communities are exactly alike. Site Surveys help quantify situational and operational characteristics.

- **Needs Survey**
  Chronic problems like father absence, poverty, and incidents of adverse childhood experiences have become commonplace. Needs Surveys can be helpful in identifying and quantifying the scale of local needs that can be addressed through Birth of a Family.

- **Demographic Survey**
  Birth of a Family is designed to be culturally attentive. Demographic Surveys help you develop deeper awareness of the people who may be involved.

Awareness

TIPS

- All three surveys are included in one single Awareness spreadsheet template.

- Strive to input the most accurate data possible.

- Cite relevant research, references, and methods used.

- Your Awareness spreadsheet will become a valuable resource that will be referenced throughout the remainder of this recipe.

SUGGESTIONS

- Go to the template package you downloaded from the Birth of a Family website.

- In the template package, locate the Awareness spreadsheet.

- Open the Awareness spreadsheet in an application such as Microsoft Excel, Apple Numbers, or Google Sheets.

- Notice that, inside the Awareness spreadsheet template, each of the three surveys already has its own individual sheet.

- Complete all three of the surveys.

- Save your work.

Well done. You just used your first template downloaded from the Birth of a Family website to develop deeper awareness about your situation and the people who may be served. The awareness you captured in your surveys will be used throughout the remainder of this recipe.

PLAN

Ingredient 3

PLAN

Noble people make noble plans and on those plans they stand.
—Isaiah 32:8

Unlike one-size-fits-all approaches, your Birth of a Family communities will be scaled and adapted to your unique situation and the people who will be served.

Your Plan will be an evidence-based framework that will:

- ◉ Inspire diligent commitment by demonstrating a logical plan

- ◉ Engage resources on a scale that is adequate to achieve stated objectives

- ◉ Adapt your Birth of a Family communities to your unique situation and to the people who will be served

Like a three-layer cake, your Birth of a Family Plan will have three sections:

- ◉ Logic

- ◉ Resources

- ◉ Adaptations

Birth
of a Family
RECIPE

INGREDIENT:

PLAN

Noble people make noble plans and on those plans they stand.

OBJECTIVE:

Create a Birth of a Family Plan that is uniquely relevant to your situation and the people you will serve.

OBJECTIVE

Create a Birth of a Family Plan that is uniquely relevant to your situation and the people you will serve.

GET STARTED

Based on your experiences seeking God first (Ingredient 1) and developing awareness Ingredient 2), plan (Ingredient 3) the creation of your new Birth of a Family communities.

> *"Noble people make noble plans and on those plans they stand."*

PLAN SECTION 1

LOGIC

TIPS

- ◎ If you have ever done any strategic planning or grant writing, you may notice features resembling logic models in the following suggestions.

- ◎ Your Birth of a Family Plan can become a powerful and useful tool.

- ◎ Once the initial draft of your Plan is done, consider having it edited and laid out by someone experienced in these fields.

- ◎ The framework for Section 1 of your Plan includes six logical categories:
  - Problem
  - Solution
  - Actions
  - Output
  - Outcomes
  - Impacts

SUGGESTIONS

- ◎ Read this entire book before you begin developing your Plan. It doesn't take that long. Understanding the recipe comprehensively before developing your Plan will enable a more proficient approach.

- ◎ Keep this book handy and open to the appropriate sections as you develop your Plan.

- ◎ Go to the template package you downloaded from the Birth of a Family website.

- ◎ From the template package, open the Plan template in a word-processing application such as Microsoft Word, Apple Pages, or Google Docs.

- ◎ Follow the instructions on the template.

- ◎ Navigate to the Logic section of the Plan template. This is where you will begin composing your Plan.

- ◎ Work through the entire framework for Section 1 of your Plan by identifying the:
  - Problem
  - Solution
  - Actions
  - Output
  - Outcomes
  - Impacts

PROBLEM

- ◎ Inside the Logic section of the Plan template, under the Problem heading, identify the problem or problems your Birth of a Family community will address.

- ◎ Consider sharing your experiences seeking and abiding in God's call to create a new Birth of a Family communities.

EXAMPLES

- The lives of pre-born children must not be taken. They are not the problem.

- Hearts of fathers turned away from their children is the leading cause of many of our most troubling issues.

- The root causes of our most troubling issues must be reached.

- The Body of Christ and life-affirming ministry are not connected the way God wants them to be connected.

Clearly identify the problem or problems your Birth of a Family community will address.

SOLUTION

- Inside the Logic section of the Plan template, under the Solution heading, explain what your Birth of a Family community will do to solve the problem you just identified.

EXAMPLE

Birth of a Family© is a proven relational-discipleship platform that has a long history of connecting fathers' hearts to their children and of connecting the Body of Christ to life-affirming ministry the way God wants them connected.

When fathers' hearts are connected to their children and the Body of Christ is connected to life-affirming ministry like God wants them connected:

- Demand for abortion goes down

- Childhood outcomes go up

- Unhealthy relationships go down

- Volunteering goes up

- Poverty, hunger, addiction, and incarceration go down
- Male involvement goes up
- Families become safer and stronger
- Stronger families contribute to stronger communities
- Earth becomes a safer place to be
- Generational and eternal change happens

Briefly and succinctly explain what your Birth of a Family communities will do to solve the problem(s) you identified.

ACTIONS

◉ Inside the Logic section of the Plan template, under the Actions heading, explain key actions that will be involved in your solution.

EXAMPLES

Key actions involved will include:

- Periodic Birth of a Family Informational Workshops that enlist, equip, and engage people of the Body of Christ in life-affirming ministry
- Regularly recurring relational-discipleship activities where people of the Body of Christ become Birth of a Family key operatives
- Inviting people to participate in recurring Birth of a Family relational-discipleship activities
- Integrating relational-discipleship into ministry models
- Developing new strategically aligned networks

- Developing and regularly evaluating new key performance indicators

- Developing new in-kind and cash support.

Explain key actions that will be involved in your solution.

OUTPUTS

⊚ Inside the Logic section of the Plan template, under the Output heading, define expected outputs. Outputs are immediate contributions to a greater outcome. Think of outputs like a homemade pie crust. The pie crust is an output. The pie is an outcome. What outputs will the application of resources cause?

EXAMPLE

Outputs (key performance indicators) will include:

- New human capital will be created.

- New events and activities will occur.

- New kinds of relational-discipleship will occur.

- More opportunities will open up for men and families to serve.

- The Body of Christ will become more connected to our pregnancy center.

- New strategically aligned networks will increase comprehensive transformation of the lives of people served by our pregnancy center.

- In-kind support will increase substantially.

Explain key actions that will be involved in your solution.

OUTCOMES

Inside the Logic section of the Plan template, under the Outcomes heading, define expected outcomes. Think of an outcome as being like a freshly baked homemade pie. The pie is the outcome. What outcomes will the outputs you just identified produce?

EXAMPLE

By connecting fathers' hearts to their children and the Body of Christ to life-affirming ministry the way God wants them to be connected:

- Capacity of our pregnancy center will increase.

- Client recidivism will decrease.

- Volunteering at our pregnancy center will increase.

- Achievement of our pregnancy-center primary strategic objectives will improve.

Define expected outcomes.

IMPACTS

- ◉ Inside the Logic section of the Plan template, under the Impacts heading, define impacts you expect. Impacts are consummate consequences and enduring, root-cause changes. Think of impacts as the lingering satisfaction of enjoying a well-made pie of which you cannot get enough.

EXAMPLE

- Impacts of our new Birth of a Family communities will include:

- Threats to pre-born lives will be reduced.

- Childhood outcomes will improve.

- Incidence of unhealthy relationships will decrease.

- Covenant-based family structures will increase.

- Fathers' hearts will be turned toward their children.

- Unprecedented engagement of the Body of Christ will occur.

- Stronger families will contribute to stronger communities.

- Generational and eternal change will happen.

- Cultures of life replace cultures of death.

- Root causes will be addressed.

Define expected impacts.

PLAN SECTION 2

RESOURCES

In this section of your Plan, you will identify the resources your new Birth of a Family communities will need.

Abiding God's call (Ingredient 1) at a level that can meet the needs (Ingredient 2) requires diligent attention to resources.

In this part of your Plan, simply identify resources without regard for their present availability or their cost. For whatever He inspires you to do, God will make a way. (Numbers 23:19)

GET STARTED

Identifying resources is nothing new. Everyone has done it. Just like any recipe, certain resources are needed in certain quantities. In this part of your Plan, you will begin by identifying the resources, and then you will be guided to estimate the quantities.

TIPS

- Don't be shy. Whoever the people, wherever the places, and whatever the things you believe are needed, be sure to include them in your Plan.

- Right now, the current availability or cost of resources doesn't matter. Just assume that God will provide, and expect Him to surprise you in the process. (Genesis 22:13)

SUGGESTIONS

- Navigate to the Resources section of the Plan template.

- Notice that, inside the Resources section of the Plan template, there are already three headings:

- People

- Places

- Things

◎ Navigate to the People heading.

◎ Notice that, under the People heading, four categories of people are already suggested:

- Visionaries and Stewards

- Participants

- Recruiters

- Key Operatives

◎ Under each of these categories, identify the human resources that will be engaged as you create your new Birth of a Family communities.

PEOPLE

VISIONARIES AND STEWARDS

Visionaries and stewards are people who share this vision (refer to the Logic part of your plan). They are people who may play key leadership roles in creating this new Birth of a Family community.

Birth of a Family communities cannot be created alone. There are a number of possibilities. Visionaries and stewards could be pastors, life-affirming ministry executives, board members and other business leaders, or social service or ministry agency leaders. They could be individuals, small-group leaders, or donors. They may also include agencies like foundations and associations.

Identify visionaries and stewards who may abide God's call with you.

TIPS

- ◉ Focus only on naming your visionary and steward roles for now. Later, in Team Build (ingredient 4 of this recipe), you will be guided in the creation of a Team Build workbook, where specific people can be identified.

SUGGESTIONS

- ◉ Navigate to the Resources section of the Plan template.

- ◉ Inside the People heading, under the Visionaries and Stewards category, identify the Visionary and Stewardship roles that apply to you and your situation.

EXAMPLES

- • Advisors, executives, and directors who might play key roles in planning, leadership, and stewardship
- • Staff assigned responsibility for various aspects of your new Birth of a Family communities. Staff roles could include roles like pregnancy-center counselors, case workers, client-service directors.

PARTICIPANTS

The term "Participants" is used to identify people who will be invited to participate in your recurring Birth of a Family relational-discipleship activities. Participants could include pregnancy-center clients, client families, referrals from other agencies and churches, peers, and family.

TIPS

- ◉ Everyone can benefit from Birth of a Family. Participants can be anyone. Pregnancy-center clients, family, friends, members of small groups, and referrals from family courts, churches, and other ministries. They can be single men and women, married or cohabiting couples, younger and older people.

- ◎ Instead of identifying specific people right now, identify general people *groups* that you may want to invite to participate in your recurring Birth of a Family relational-discipleship activities.

- ◎ Later, in Team Build (Ingredient 4), you will estimate how many people might accept the invitation to become Participants in your recurring Birth of a Family relational-discipleship activities.

SUGGESTIONS

- ◎ Navigate to the Resources section of the Plan template.

- ◎ Inside the People heading, under the Participants category, identify people and people groups that you want to be invited or referred to participate in your recurring Birth of a Family relational-discipleship activities.

EXAMPLES

- Through life-affirming ministries, God has created a gateway into the lives of people who may otherwise be inaccessible to the Body of Christ. By building relationships and rapport with people who are seeking their services, life-affirming ministries make it possible for the Body of Christ to connect with people who might otherwise never seek church support.[8]

- When appropriate and safe, we will invite our clients to our recurring Birth of a Family relational-discipleship activities.

- People may be referred to participate in our recurring Birth of a Family relational-discipleship activities by:
  - Churches and pastors
  - Family courts and child-protective services
  - Other ministries
  - Active and former Participants

---

8 https://research.lifeway.com/2015/11/23/women-distrust-church-on-abortion/

RECRUITERS

Recruiters are people who invite or refer people to participate in your Birth of a Family relational-discipleship activities. Recruiters can be pregnancy-center counselors, pastors, and select social-service agencies.

TIPS

- Because pregnancy-center counselors are often the first to develop relationships with pregnancy-center clients, they can become super recruiters.
- Engaging pastors and churches as recruiters deepens the connection between the Body of Christ and life-affirming ministry.
- Engaging select social-service agencies as recruiters can increase the number of people exposed to life-affirming ministry.

SUGGESTIONS

- Navigate to the Resources section of the Plan template.
- Inside the People heading, under the Recruiters category, identify people and agencies that can help you invite or refer people to participate in the Birth of a Family relational-discipleship activities.

KEY OPERATIVES

"Give me a lever long enough and a fulcrum on which to place it, and I shall move the world."
—Archimedes

Key Operatives are volunteers who serve in key operational roles in your new Birth of a Family communities. Key Operatives almost always include Birth of a Family Coordinators, Facilitators, and Mentors. Typically, the addition of Key Operatives doubles the number of active volunteers and substantially increases male involvement within the first year of new Birth of a Family communities.

Best practices include having Coordinators and Facilitators on board early in the process of creating new Birth of a Family communities.

BIRTH OF A FAMILY COORDINATORS

Birth of a Family Coordinators are like event planners. They plan for and coordinate activities, people, places, and things involved in your new Birth of a Family communities. Typically, Coordinators:

- Have access to and appropriately share Birth of a Family resources with team members

- Coordinate all Birth of a Family events and activities

- Maintain contact information for everyone involved in our Birth of a Family communities

- Capture and input our key performance indicators

- Receive referrals from pregnancy-center counselors and others

- Invite referrals to participate in our recurring Birth of a Family relational-discipleship activities

- Report metrics and concerns

Helpful characteristics for Birth of a Family Coordinators can include:

- Communication skills

- Digital-device and application skills

- Resourcefulness

- Planning and organizational skills

- Teamwork

- Problem-solving

- Social-media skills

BIRTH OF A FAMILY FACILITATORS

Birth of a Family Facilitators are trained volunteers who facilitate recurring Birth of a Family relational-discipleship activities. From time to time, they may also facilitate training and Informational Workshops.

Family Facilitators may work as teams or individuals and can be men, women, couples, or families.

The role of Birth of a Family Facilitators involves cultivating relational dialogue during recurring Birth of a Family relational-discipleship activities where people can experience role modeling, mentoring, and support.

While other resources can be used during recurring Birth of a Family relational-discipleship activities, Let's Talk: Relational Discipleship Conversation Guides[9] is often the primary resource used.

Key Operatives such as Birth of a Family Facilitators are typically enlisted, equipped, and engaged during our Birth of a Family Informational Workshops.

Birth of a Family Facilitators typically:

- Are available for a specified number of recurring Birth of a Family relational-discipleship activities

- Maintain a courteous environment during activities

- Capture and report key performance indicators to our Birth of a Family Coordinator(s)

- Encourage Christlike concern for all people

- Emphasize Biblical fundamentals

- Report all concerns regarding Birth of a Family

- Facilitate strategic network connections

Helpful characteristics for our Birth of a Family Facilitators can include:

- Patience

- Listening skills

---

9 "Let's Talk: Relational Discipleship Conversation Guides," Stuart Carver, *ReGen Creative*, Feb 15, 2023, available at amazon.com

- Adaptability and creativity

- Resourcefulness

- Wisdom

- Humility

- A good sense of humor

BIRTH OF A FAMILY MENTORS

Birth of a Family Mentors can be men, women, and couples who have been enlisted, equipped, and engaged to join Participants and Facilitators during recurring Birth of a Family activities. Mentors are available to role model, mentor, and support as needed.

Mentor roles can be appropriate for men, women, couples, and families, younger and older.

Birth of a Family Mentors are most often enlisted, equipped, and engaged during Birth of a Family Informational Workshops. Mentors typically:

- Birth of a Family Mentors typically are available for a specified number of recurring Birth of a Family relational-discipleship activities

- Maintain a courteous demeanor during activities

- Communicate conversationally

- Demonstrate Christlike concern for all people

- Emphasize biblical fundamentals

- Report all concerns regarding Birth of a Family

- Facilitate strategic network connections

Five golden rules for Key Operatives include:

◉ Show up. In other words, be consistently present. Even if no Participants show up, continue your pilot series of Birth of a Family activities. If you build a sustainable Birth of a Family community, people will come.

◉ Be nice. In other words, ensure a welcoming, congenial atmosphere during your Birth of a Family activities.

◉ Show no condemnation. People involved in your Birth of a Family activities will be diverse. Ensure Christlike concern for all people.

◉ Speak truth in love. In other words, ensuring Christlike love for others is what opens doors for truth.

◉ Offer biblically grounded role modeling, mentoring, and support. In other words, promote relational-discipleship that is consistent with God's word, not the ways of this world.

TIPS

◉ New Key Operative roles are appropriate for men, women, and families, younger and older.

◉ Include Key Operative roles such as Birth of a Family Coordinators, Facilitators, and Mentors. The numbers of and names of specific people can be added later in Team Building (Ingredient 4 in this recipe)

SUGGESTIONS

◉ Navigate to the Resources section of the Plan template.

◉ Inside the People heading, under the Key Operatives category, define Key Operative roles you want to include in your new Birth of a Family communities.

◉ Notice that these three Key Operative roles already appear in the Key Operatives category:

- Birth of a Family Coordinators

- Birth of a Family Facilitators

- Birth of a Family Mentors

◎ Add other Key Operative roles as needed. Examples of additional roles could include case workers and managers, mental-health counselors, grant writers, and participant advocates.

You've just identified some of the *people* who can be involved in your new Birth of a Family communities. Save your work. Revisit your Resources periodically to refine.

Next, you will identify *places* you need for your Birth of a Family events and activities.

PLACES

Birth of a Family events and activities can happen virtually anywhere, including homes, churches, pregnancy centers, and casual meeting places like coffee shops, cafes, and even online.

OBJECTIVE
Identify the best places where your Birth of a Family events and activities will occur.

GET STARTED
Places are needed for at least two types of Birth of a Family events and activities:

◎ Periodic Birth of a Family Informational Workshops, where people are enlisted, equipped, and engaged to serve as Coordinators, Facilitators, and Mentors

◎ Recurring Birth of a Family activities, where Participants, Facilitators, and Mentors regularly gather to experience relational-discipleship together.

Periodic Birth of a Family Informational Workshops should occur in places that can accommodate larger groups. Consider larger rooms, conference rooms, and spaces that have media capabilities.

Places for Birth of a Family relational-discipleship activities do not need to be large but must accommodate interactive conversation and relational-discipleship. For both of these kinds of activities, childcare may be a consideration.

A best practice over the years has involved cooperating with churches that have both large and small spaces, and that sometimes offer childcare as well. As a bonus, churches can also provide places and services for Participant weddings and baptisms.

TIPS

- There are lots of great places. Use the best places available.

- Adapt spaces to encourage open dialogue and relational-discipleship.

- Make places easy to locate.

- Choose places that are safe, well-lit, and accessible.

SUGGESTIONS

- Navigate to the Resources section of the Plan template.

- Navigate to the Places heading of your Plan.

- Identify at least one specific place where you would like for your periodic Birth of a Family Informational Workshops to occur.

- Next, identify at least one specific place you would like for your recurring Birth of a Family relational-discipleship activities to occur.

EXAMPLES

Churches often provide places for Birth of a Family Informational Workshops, typically in places that can accommodate larger audiences and include seating, furnishing, restrooms, and presentation equipment. Sometimes, childcare and food services are also provided.

Recurring Birth of a Family relational-discipleship activities typically occur in places that are more suited to small-group conversation.

Great progress. You have prepared for the best places where your Birth of a Family events and activities will occur. Next, prepare for the Things you need.

THINGS

If they are not people or places, consider them things.

OBJECTIVE

Identify things you need for your Birth of a Family communities. Things can include:

- Workspaces, furnishings, equipment, and supplies
- Money
- **Let's Talk: Relational Discipleship Conversation Guides**[10]
- Communications devices and plans
- Amenities for events and activities
- Childcare
- Marketing and media
- Strategically aligned networks

GET STARTED

Identify anything you believe will help you create and sustain your new Birth of a Family communities.

---

10 "Let's Talk: Relational Discipleship Conversation Guides," Stuart Carver, *ReGen Creative*, Feb 15, 2023, available at amazon.com

⦿ Don't worry about cost right now. Simply identify things that you believe will help you create and sustain your newly added capacity and excellence to your new Birth of a Family communities. Ways to acquire things will be addressed later, in Optimize (Ingredient 6 of this recipe)

SUGGESTIONS

⦿ Navigate to the Resources section of the Plan template.

⦿ Inside the Resources section of your Plan, navigate to the Things heading.

⦿ Under the Things heading, identify things you believe will help you create and sustain your newly added capacity and excellence to your new Birth of a Family communities.

PLAN SECTION 3

ADAPT

Broad adaptability and scalability make it possible to create locally relevant Birth of a Family communities anywhere in the world.

> *"Broad adaptability and scalability make it possible to create locally relevant Birth of a Family communities anywhere in the world."*

Adaptability is essential to cutting-edge success in faith-based ministry in this day and age. The Birth of a Family recipe doesn't just *allow* adaptation, it *thrives* on it.

Birth of a Family causes relational-discipleship. Consider the implications.

- ◎ Client experiences will be expanded and extended
- ◎ New opportunities will open up
- ◎ More volunteers will be involved
- ◎ Male involvement will increase substantially
- ◎ Deeper needs will be met
- ◎ The Body of Chrrist will be more connected
- ◎ Time, energy, and resources will need to be allocated to relational-discipleship activities

Think about adaptations that may need to be considered in light of these Birth of a Family realities.

OBJECTIVE
Adapt your new Birth of a Family communities to fit your unique situation and the unique people who will be served.

GET STARTED
When compared to one-size-fits-all approaches, adaptation to local situations and specific people is a distinctive feature of Birth of a Family. Make your new Birth of a Family communities fit your unique situation and the unique people who will be served.

What adaptations may need to be considered in light of these Birth of a Family realities?

TIPS

- ◎ Dream as big as God wants you to. (John 15:7)
- ◎ Embrace adaptation as essential to cutting-edge success.

> *"Dream as big as God wants you to."*

SUGGESTIONS

- ⊙ Navigate to the Adapt section of your Plan.

- ⊙ In the Adapt section of your Plan, define adaptations you want to consider as you create your new Birth of a Family communities.

Well done! You have just created your own unique Birth of a Family Plan. Birth of a Family Plans are not perfect predictions. They are thoughtful preparations.

Plans can and sometimes should change. Save your work. Revisit your plan occasionally. As you learn and grow, continue using your Plan to abide God's call with excellence. During the next part of the Birth of a Family recipe, you will build your team.

> *Plans are not perfect predictions. They are thoughtful preparations.*

TEAM BUILD

Ingredient 4

TEAM BUILD

With good ingredients, it's hard to go very wrong.

Team building is to Birth of a Family what good ingredients are to a great recipe. One of the most common comments from people involved in Birth of a Family teams goes something like this: "Nothing like this has happened before." New Birth of a Family teams create new capacities to do new things and create new impacts.

Team Building is your opportunity to respond in a manner that is of sufficient scale to accomplish your goals and God's desire. (Matthew 28:19-20)

In many respects, connecting fathers' hearts to their children and the Body of Christ to life-affirming ministry boils down to one thing—scale. When enough fathers' hearts are turned and enough people of the Body of Christ become front-runners instead of bystanders, life-saving connections will be made.

Team Building is an ongoing process, not a one-time event. It is a habit, a culture, an attitude. As your Birth of a Family communities grow, new team opportunities will continuously

---

Birth
of a Family
RECIPE

INGREDIENT:

TEAM BUILD

With good ingredients, it's hard to go very wrong.

OBJECTIVE:

Engage people in sufficient scale to accomplish your goals and God's desire.

open up. The bottom line is this. The ultimate key to your sustainability is continuously increasing the number and capacities of people involved. In this way, you will respond in a manner that is of sufficient scale to accomplish your goals and God's desire.

OBJECTIVE

Engage people in sufficient scale to accomplish your goals and God's desire.

GET STARTED

- ⊙ What is the appropriate scale?

- ⊙ How many people of the Body of Christ do you need to enlist, equip, and engage?

- ⊙ How will you engage these people in your Birth of a Family communities?

This special recipe includes a three-part process to build your new Birth of a Family team.

SCALE

- ⊙ Recruit

- ⊙ Engage

- ⊙ Scale

> *"New Birth of a Family teams create new capacities to do new things and create new impacts."*

When you're baking a cake, the proportions of the ingredients in the recipe are determined by the size of the cake.

One number is used as a baseline to determine the starting scale of your new Birth of a Family communities. That number is how many people might accept the invitation to be Participants in your recurring Birth of a Family relational-discipleship activities.

TIPS

- A reasonable estimate is all you need to scale your Birth of a Family teams. Once you have an estimate of how many people might accept the invitation to be Participants in your recurring Birth of a Family relational-discipleship activities, you can build your Birth of a Family teams.

- Example. For pregnancy centers, a reasonable estimate is that about 25% of the total number of unique clients being regularly served will accept the invitation to be Participants in your recurring Birth of a Family relational-discipleship activities. In other words, if a pregnancy center is regularly serving 40 unique clients a month, then it would be reasonable to estimate that 10 of them might accept the invitation to be Participants in your recurring Birth of a Family relational-discipleship activities.

- Example. For other types of small groups, it would be reasonable to estimate that all group members might participate in Birth of a Family relational-discipleship activities.

SUGGESTIONS

- Go to the template package you downloaded from the Birth of a Family website.

- From the template package, open the Team Build workbook template in a spreadsheet application such as Microsoft Excel, Apple Numbers, or Google Sheets.

- Notice that the Team Build workbook template already includes individual sheets for the roles Visionaries and Directors, Participants, Pregnancy Center Counselors, and Key Operatives.

- Open the Participants sheet in your Team Build workbook.

- At the top of the Participants sheet, in the space to the right of the word "Scale," enter the number of people you estimate will accept the invitation to be Participants in your recurring Birth of a

Family relational-discipleship activities. This number is the baseline for scaling the rest of your Birth of a Family teams.

- ◉ Open the Pregnancy Center Counselors sheet in your Team Build workbook.

- ◉ At the top of the Pregnancy Center Counselors sheet, in the field labeled "Scale," enter the number of Pregnancy Center Counselors who currently interact with your clients. If you're using Birth of a Family as a small-group experience, this sheet may not be applicable.

- ◉ Open the Key Operatives sheet in your Team Build workbook.

- ◉ Under the heading "Coordinators," in the space to the right of the word "Scale," enter the number of Birth of a Family Coordinators you would like to engage.

  - Rule of thumb: For every twenty people you estimate will accept the invitation to be Participants in your recurring Birth of a Family relational-discipleship activities, add one Coordinator.

- ◉ In the Key Operatives sheet in your Team Build workbook, under the heading "Facilitators," in the space to the right of the word "Scale," enter the number of Birth of a Family Facilitators you would like to engage.

  - Rule of thumb: For every twenty people you estimate will accept the invitation to be Participants in your recurring Birth of a Family relational-discipleship activities, add two Facilitators.

- ◉ In the Key Operatives sheet in your Team Build workbook, under the heading "Mentors," in the space to the right of the word "Scale," enter the number of Birth of a Family Mentors you would like to engage.

  - Rule of thumb: For every person you estimate will accept the invitation to be a Participant in your recurring Birth of a Family relational-discipleship activities, add one Mentor.

- ◉ Your creativity and customization are encouraged as you build your Birth of a Family team. Adapt the template to your satisfaction.

EXAMPLES

50 Unique Clients Regularly Served Monthly

A pregnancy center regularly serving an average of 50 unique clients (mothers) per month can reasonably estimate a scale where:

- It is reasonable to estimate twelve clients might accept the invitation to be Participants in recurring Birth of a Family relational-discipleship activities. This becomes the baseline for scaling the rest of this Birth of a Family team.

- With this baseline of twelve potential Participants in mind:
  - At least one Birth of a Family Coordinator is needed
  - At least two Birth of a Family Facilitators are needed
  - At least twelve Birth of a Family Mentors are needed

A Hundred Unique Clients Regularly Served Monthly

A pregnancy center serving an average of a hundred unique clients (mothers) per month can reasonably estimate a scale where:

- With the baseline of twenty-five potential Participants in mind:
  - At least two Birth of a Family Coordinators are needed
  - At least four Birth of a Family Facilitators are needed
  - At least twenty-five Birth of a Family Mentors are needed.

A small group with twelve regularly attending members

A small group with twelve regularly attending members can reasonably estimate a scale where:

- All twelve group members will accept the invitation to be Participants in recurring Birth of a Family relational-discipleship activities

- With the baseline of twelve potential Participants in mind:
  - At least one Birth of a Family Coordinator is needed

  - At least two Birth of a Family Facilitators are needed
  - At least twelve Birth of a Family Mentors are needed

Birth of a Family is not a curricular approach, where one speaker lectures many. It is a relational-discipleship approach, where many help each other turn toward God and His ways.

While there is no stratification or official designation of people participating in Birth of a Family relational-discipleship activities, some people are participating because they need relational-discipleship. On the other hand, Birth of a Family Facilitators and Mentors are participating because they want to respectfully offer relational-discipleship.

This is a key distinction between Birth of a Family and other types of curricular approaches. The primary purpose for participation is not learning. The primary purpose is experiencing relational-discipleship, role modeling, mentoring, and support. That is why serving twelve Participants requires twelve or more Birth of a Family Key Operatives. This dynamic feature of Birth of a Family makes it possible to respond in a manner that is of sufficient scale to accomplish your goals and God's desire.

RECRUIT

Responding in a manner that is of sufficient scale to accomplish your goals and God's desire requires a whole new level of recruitment.

Birth of a Family Informational Workshops can be used repeatedly to recruit people in your new Birth of a Family communities. These hour-and-a-half workshops inform, train, and invite people to serve in the Birth of a Family roles you identified in your Plan. This single workshop has been sufficient to recruit many great Birth of a Family teams of adequate scale.

TIPS

- A Birth of a Family Informational Workshop sample is included in the template package that is available for download from the Birth of a Family website.

- The Birth of a Family Informational Workshop sample can be used as is, customized to your preferences, or as a guide to create your own workshop presentation.

- People are enlisted by being invited to attend the workshop.

- People are equipped by being informed about what Birth of a Family is, how it works, and why it is needed during the workshop.

- People are engaged by being invited to sign up to serve in Birth of a Family roles before they leave the workshop. (Isaiah 6:8)

SUGGESTIONS

- Open the Birth of a Family Informational Workshop sample in a presentation application such as Microsoft PowerPoint, Apple Keynote, or Google Slides.

- Review the entire presentation.

- Customize the workshop to your preferences.

- Add your own branding and information about your group or agency to the workshop presentation.

- Practice. Use your workshop presentation and your Plan to introduce your new Birth of a Family communities. Consider sharing with other Visionaries, executive teams, staff, volunteers, pastors, and donors.

- Use it. These workshops have been more effective than any other strategy in recruiting people into Birth of a Family communities.

- As your Birth of a Family communities grow, share your success stories in your workshop presentation.

- Use your workshop presentation in person and online.

- Make your workshop presentation available on your website.

EXAMPLE

- Set dates for your Birth of a Family Informational Workshops.

- Choose appropriate venues.

- Consider ways to make your venues clean, orderly, inviting, and easy to find.

- Plan for two-hour workshops.

- Pray for your workshops while you plan.

- Engage presenters.

- Engage event-planning teams.

- Engage people to welcome and register guests.

- Practice the presentation.

- Invite pastors, churches, donors, directors, small-group leaders, and other ministry leaders.

- Pray for your events while they are happening.

- Pray for the people present at your workshops.

- Publicize your workshops in all of your routine marketing channels.

- Start and finish your workshops exactly on time.

- Take breaks every thirty minutes.

- Reserve fifteen minutes for questions and answers.

- Ask people to volunteer to join your Birth of a Family team before closing your workshops.

- Collect names, contact information, and preferences from people who want to join your Birth of a Family team.

- Tell people who want to join your Birth of a Family team exactly what to expect next.

- Provide ways for attendants to evaluate your workshops.

- Give God thanks for calling laborers into the harvest.

ENGAGE

Fresh ingredients have shelf life. In other words, if they don't get used promptly, they get stale. Once people are recruited, it is vital to engage them in meaningful, well-planned work as soon as possible. Activating new volunteers within fifteen days is best; within thirty days can work, but, after forty days, they are probably beyond their expiration date.

To help preserve the fresh enthusiasm of the people you recruit to join your Birth of a Family teams, keep the dates for your Birth of a Family Informational Workshops close to the dates when your recurring Birth of a Family relational-discipleship activities are going to begin. Just like you might grocery-shop the day before for a special meal, a little calendar coordination is all that is needed.

OBJECTIVE

Populate your Birth of a Family Team.

GET STARTED

As you recruit people, some will sign up. When they do, use your Team Build workbook to assign them roles on your team.

TIPS

- ⊚ Your Team Build workbook can help you:
  - Be a good steward of the laborers God is sending you

  - Assign roles

  - Communicate with your team

  - Honor time commitments of your team members

  - Anticipate team needs

  - Know the value of human-capital investment in your Birth of a Family communities

SUGGESTIONS

- ⊚ Open your Team Build workbook

- ⊚ Notice that the Team Build workbook already includes individual sheets for the roles of Visionaries and Directors, Participants, Pregnancy Center Counselors, and Key Operatives.

- ⊚ Inside your Team Build workbook, on the sheet for Key Operatives, there are three headings: Coordinators, Facilitators, and Mentors.

- ⊚ On the Key Operatives sheet, under the heading "Coordinators," enter the information for each individual person serving in a Coordinator role in your Birth of a Family communities.

- ⊚ On the Key Operatives sheet, under the heading "Facilitators," enter the information for each individual person serving in a Facilitator role in your Birth of a Family communities.

- ⊚ On the Key Operatives sheet, under the heading "Mentor," enter the information for each individual person serving in a Mentor role in your Birth of a Family communities.

- ◉ As more and more people are recruited, add them to your Birth of a Family team.

- ◉ Add new categories as needed.

- ◉ Repeat often.

People and relationships are, by far, the most important elements in your new Birth of a Family communities. Use your Team Build workbook to honor team-member commitments, anticipate your team needs, and to demonstrate the value of human-capital investment in your Birth of a Family communities.

The next ingredient in the Birth of a Family recipe is Diligence.

DILIGENCE

Ingredient 5

DILIGENCE

Persistent work carefully done.

Like the pleasant aroma of vanilla that fills the room when the cap is removed, persistent work that is carefully done infuses a culture of diligence into your Birth of a Family communities. You will learn how to infuse diligence in this part of the recipe.

Before getting into the "how to," it is vital to share what has been learned over the years about how diligence is related to the sustainability of new Birth of a Family communities. The 2017 evaluation of Birth of a Family proved that commitment, not a perfect plan, is the key factor in achieving sustainability.

Complex problems addressed by Birth of a Family are not easily solved. Connecting fathers' hearts to their children and the Body of Christ to life-affirming ministry the way God wants them to be connected are easy ideas to like, but even the best ideas aren't good enough. Persistent work carefully done is what it takes to make these connections. (Matthew 7:20)

The infusion of diligence into well-conceived plans is a classic challenge that can be a struggle even for leading global agencies. Sometimes referred to as "actionizing strategy," planning to do

---

Birth of a Family RECIPE

INGREDIENT:

DILIGENCE

Diligence is persistent work carefully done.

OBJECTIVE:

Stimulate a culture of diligence by setting dates and commissioning work.

great things is far more common than actually getting great things done. (James 1:23-25) As yeast is to the bread, diligence becomes the transformational ingredient that precipitates results. (Matthew 7:20)

OBJECTIVE
Stimulate a culture of diligence by setting dates and commissioning work.

GET STARTED
Set dates and commission work.

SET DATES
Just the mere act of setting a timer to know when to take a cake out of the oven inspires diligence.

> *"Stimulate a culture of diligence by setting dates and commissioning work."*

GET STARTED
Setting dates triggers diligence. People say, "This is really going to happen! What do we need to do?"

TIPS

- Choosing the date range that you want your recurring Birth of a Family relational-discipleship activities to occur is a good place to start.

- A series of at least twelve consecutive Birth of a Family relational-discipleship activities is ideal.

> *"Setting dates triggers diligence. People say, 'This is really going to happen!'"*

- First rounds of Birth of a Family relational-discipleship activities are often referred to as "pilot activities."

- A limited round of pilot activities is sometimes easier for new volunteers to manage.

- At least twelve consecutive Birth of a Family relational-discipleship activities are needed to produce measurable results that can later be evaluated.

- With this date range in mind, you can set all the other dates you need.

- Having this date set allows you to let Facilitators and Mentors know when they are needed.

- Setting this date range will drive preparation for your recurring Birth of a Family relational-discipleship activities.

- Develop the habit of setting dates.

SUGGESTIONS

- Open your calendar.

- Determine how many recurring Birth of a Family relational-discipleship activities you want to have in your initial pilot.

- Set the date range for when you want your first round of recurring Birth of a Family relational-discipleship activities to begin.

- Set the date and time for each recurring Birth of a Family relational-discipleship activity occurring during the date range you just determined.

- The date that your very first Birth of a Family relational-discipleship activity occurs now becomes your start date. Using your start date, you can now set dates for the preparations that need to occur.

- Working backwards at least six weeks from your start date, set the date to onboard your first Birth of a Family Coordinator. Onboarding your Birth of a Family Coordinator at least six weeks prior to your start date will give Coordinators time to:

  • Develop your Birth of a Family database

- Receive referrals from Pregnancy Center Counselors

- Schedule Birth of a Family Informational Workshops

- Arrange venues for workshops and recurring Birth of a Family relational-discipleship activities

- Coordinate amenities and provisions for events and activities

◉ Working backwards at least four weeks from your start date, set the date to begin inviting Participants to experience your recurring Birth of a Family activities. Beginning to invite Participants to experience your recurring Birth of a Family activities about four weeks in advance of your start date will give them enough notice, without making them wait too long.

◉ Working backwards no more than four weeks from your start date, set the date to host your first Birth of a Family Informational Workshop. This workshop is where you will enlist, equip, and engage your Birth of a Family Facilitators and Mentors.

◉ Set a date for your first evaluation of your new Birth of a Family communities to occur. Ideally, this date will be within two weeks after your first pilot series of recurring Birth of a Family relational-discipleship activities.

There will be many other dates you will set.

- Sometimes those dates will involve meetings with team members, pastors, donors, and networkers.

- After your pilot series of recurring Birth of a Family activities, you will set dates for more.

- Occasionally, you will need to set dates for additional Birth of a Family Informational Workshops to enlist, equip, and engage more people.

Setting dates is a habit you can cultivate to infuse your Birth of a Family communities with a culture of diligence.

COMMISSION WORK

Like setting dates, commissioning work ignites a culture of diligence. Enthusiastic people with no assignments are like cooks in a restaurant with no patrons to serve. Commissioning work has an inspirational effect on enthusiastic people. Strive for a quantum leap of engagement by commissioning the work.

GET STARTED

Commissioning well-planned work that makes a difference is a leading factor in sustainable movements. Give people meaningful, well-planned work to do in your Birth of a Family communities.

> *"Strive for a quantum leap of engagement by commissioning the work."*

TIPS

- ◉ Birth of a Family is a proven platform for commissioning people as the key catalysts of change.

- ◉ Influential roles are integral to Birth of a Family.

- ◉ Birth of a Family produces meaningful work.

- ◉ Your Birth of a Family Plan is a good plan for work that makes a difference.

- ◉ Develop the habit of engaging people.

SUGGESTIONS

- ◉ Open your Team Build workbook.

- ◉ Inside your Team Build workbook, there are individual sheets for the roles of Visionaries, Directors, Participants, Pregnancy Center Counselors, and Key Operatives.

- ◉ On these individual sheets inside your Team Build workbook, beside each person's name and contact info, there is space to commission specific work.

◉ Commission work by having conversations with each person on your Birth of a Family team. Help them learn more about their roles and opportunities. Learn about their expectations, concerns, and needs. Then, accordingly assign them meaningful work.

Commissioning people to perform the work is a habit you can cultivate to infuse your Birth of a Family communities with a culture of diligence.

EXAMPLES

Visionaries and Stewards

Commission Visionaries and Stewards with the work of:
- Inspiring and appreciating your Birth of a Family teams
- Developing volunteer, in-kind, and cash support for your Birth of a Family communities.

Participants

Commission Participants with the work of:
- Participating in 70% or more of your recurring Birth of a Family relational-discipleship activities
- Developing their own individual action plans
- Getting them the help they need

Pregnancy Center Counselors

Commission Pregnancy Center Counselors with the work of:
- Inviting clients to participate in your recurring Birth of a Family relational-discipleship activities
- Reporting any concerns they may have
- Participating in evaluations of your Birth of a Family communities

Coordinators

Commission Coordinators with the work of:

- Compiling and reporting key performance indicators
- Participating in evaluations of your Birth of a Family communities
- Suggesting special events to celebrate milestones and accomplishments
- Recruiting new people onto your Birth of a Family teams
- Developing strategic alliances

Facilitators

Commission Facilitators with the work of:

- Evaluating meeting venues and times
- Recruiting new people onto your Birth of a Family teams
- Presenting your Birth of a Family Informational Workshops
- Reporting on the progress of your recurring Birth of a Family relational-discipleship activities
- Reporting any concerns they may have
- Participating in evaluations of your Birth of a Family communities

Mentors

Commission Mentors with the work of:

- Recruiting new people onto your Birth of a Family teams
- Participating in evaluations of your Birth of a Family communities
- Facilitating Birth of a Family relational-discipleship activities as needed
- Reporting any concerns they may have

There are just two more ingredients in this special recipe: Optimize and Evaluate.

OPTIMIZE

Ingredient 6

OPTIMIZE

Optimization is planned excellence.

Birth of a Family provides a trustworthy platform from which to courageously optimize. Because it is a proven approach with a clear, consistent recipe, you can optimize with confidence.

OBJECTIVE

Optimize Birth of a Family to be effective in your unique situation and with the unique people being served.

GET STARTED

One of the last things you do with a great recipe is arrange it beautifully on the plate. In the optimize ingredient in this recipe, the objective is to add those final crowning touches that take your new Birth of a Family communities from good to great. All it takes to go from good to great is an ambitious appetite to excel.

TIPS

- ◎ Most optimizations lie just beyond the status quo.
- ◎ Some optimizations require a little extra effort. Others require a lot of extra effort.

> **Birth of a Family RECIPE**
>
> **INGREDIENT:**
>
> ## OPTIMIZE
>
> Optimzation is planned excellence.
>
> **OBJECTIVE:**
>
> Optimize Birth of a Family to be especially effective in your situation and with the people being served.

- ◉ Optimizing is never risk free.

- ◉ Optimize like Jesus optimized—toward the most oppressed and least served. (Isaiah 58:6-12)

SUGGESTIONS

- ◉ In your situation, what three things are most debilitating to the people that will be served by your Birth of a Family communities? Consider your Needs and Demographic Surveys.

- ◉ If you could have anything you wanted for the people who will be served by your Birth of a Family communities, what would it be? Name three.

- ◉ Using your answers to these two questions, what possible optimizations come to mind for your Birth of a Family communities?

- ◉ To integrate optimizations, revisit the Adapt section of your Birth of a Family Plan.

Family

Threats to pre-born lives are, first and foremost, a family issue.

Since human beings first walked on the moon, the world population has doubled and will top 10 billion soon. Procreation is at an all-time high, while the family cycle is plummeting into an abyss.

Carle Clark Zimmerman was a historian and Harvard University sociologist who studied the rise and fall of empires in world history. In his book *Family and Civilization*,[11] published in 1947, Carle correlated the disintegration of various cultures with the parallel decline of family structures. Eight progressive dysfunctions were correlated with the demise of those cultures:

- • Decline in covenant marriage
- • Male absence from roles in home, church, and community

---

11 Carle C. Zimmerman, *Family and Civilization* Edited by James Kurth. Wilmington, DE: ISI Books, 2008. ISBN-10: 1933859377; ISBN-13: 978–1933859378

- Expanded female roles in home, church, and community
- Diminished value of family
- Juvenile delinquency, promiscuity, and rebellion
- Traditional roles and responsibilities rejected
- Commonplace infidelity
- Intensifying sexual perversions

The family cycle is the most powerful cycle on Earth. Regardless of what else may be going on in the world, all people are a part of the family cycle. Nothing shapes the human experience like family does.

Outside of God's ways, procreation has become the catalyst of a frightening epidemic, an epidemic that will not simply self-correct. Specialized intervention is necessary—in other words, optimization.

Because of their proximity to family, life-affirming ministry and the Body of Christ are both uniquely situated to positively impact family experiences. Pursuing this optimization in unity is, without question, the best, fastest way to reach the real root causes of many of our most disturbing problems.

TRUE CASE STUDIES

Optimizing to promote covenant-based family structures

In 2008, growing numbers of Birth of a Family Participants were transitioning into covenant-based marriage relationships. A specialized network was developed to make Biblical covenant marriages easy, affordable, and fun.

- Birth of a Family Participants in Florida were able to receive a 50% discount on their marriage licenses.

- A pastor was engaged by these Birth of a Family communities to officiate at weddings and baptisms.

- A church provided the venue for free. Birth of a Family Coordinators, Facilitators, and Mentors served as event planners.

- A local store helped with formal wedding attire.

The results included dozens of Biblical covenant weddings for people who otherwise would likely have continued their traditions of single parenting, cohabiting, and cycles of unhealthy relationships. Many were not just married—they were baptized, too.

TRUE CASE STUDY

Optimizing to promote Biblical manhood, husbandry, and fatherhood
This true-case study involves a number of fathers of children carried by women who were clients of a pregnancy center. After participating in recurring Birth of a Family relational-discipleship activities for some time, these fathers developed a specialized network that promoted Biblical manhood, husbandry, and fatherhood. It was a small group they called "Quest," in which other fathers like themselves experienced unprecedented change.

TRUE CASE STUDY

Optimizing to help single-parent families achieve sustainable jobs, housing, and transportation
A small Birth of a Family community specializes in helping single parents and families achieve sustainable jobs, transportation, and housing. They once helped a single mother with five children purchase a four-bedroom home on a one-acre lot. House payments were one half the amount this family previously paid in rent. They acquired more than $60,000 in equity the day they moved in. Once she established home ownership, the mother was able to finance the purchase of a reliable used car, the mother will soon graduate from nursing school, and they haven't moved again since.

TRUE CASE STUDY

Optimizing to meet mental-health needs
Examining the most challenging needs Participants were facing, a multi-site Birth of a Family community discovered a desperate need for professional mental-health counseling. Negotiating with three area

counselors, they formed an agreement that resulted in the availability of 240 counseling appointments per year. Counselors provided services for half price. Participants paid a $10 co-pay per appointment, and donors funded a proposal to cover the balance of the cost.

TRUE CASE STUDY

Optimizing to connect donors to the values added by Birth of a Family
The creation and continuance of many new Birth of a Family communities have been fully funded. Donors want to fund evidence-based solutions that reach the root of the problem.

Visionaries and Stewards of a Florida pregnancy center wanted to create their own Birth of a Family communities, but they needed it to be fully funded. Using their Plan, they created a proposal that was shared with a donor network. The donor network funded not only the creation cost of $16,503 but also continued fully funding subsequent Birth of a Family activities at $10,000 a year for almost a decade.

The fundamentals of the Birth of a Family recipe are consistently good. Informed, creative optimization will transform your new Birth of a Family communities from good to great.

EVALUATION

Ingredient 7

EVALUATION

The results of *Birth of a Family are valuable.* The final ingredient in the Birth of a Family recipe is Evaluation. There's much more to evaluation than just finding out if Birth of a Family works. The purpose of this vital ingredient includes:

- Proving progress with evidence

- Discovering opportunities to increase impact

- Avoiding threats and weaknesses

- Establishing tangible and monetary value of Birth of a Family outcomes

EXAMPLES

- Since 2006, over half of Birth of a Family Participants say that the experience has turned them toward God and His ways for their families.

- Volunteering almost always doubles where new Birth of a Family communities are created.

Birth
of a Family
RECIPE

INGREDIENT:

EVALUATION

Taste and see that Yahweh is good.

OBJECTIVE:

Experience Birth of a Family firsthand. Encounter the fruit. Tell the story.

- The in-kind value of Birth of a Family volunteers often exceeds $30,000 annually.

- Each father's heart turned toward their children saves local, state, and federal governments more than $25,000 annually.

You've been cooking! The table has been set. You sought God first and committed to abide by His extraordinary call to connect fathers' hearts to their children and to connect the Body of Christ to life-affirming ministry the way God wants them to be connected.

The deeper awareness you developed using your surveys empowered you to create an inspiring Plan that engages the Body

> *"The table has been set."*

of Christ in life-affirming ministry like never before. With a team built, dates set, and work commissioned, the time has come to experience the fruit of your labors.

The question, "Will it work?" must have crossed your mind. History speaks for itself. The Birth of a Family recipe works. Now it's time to prove it works for you. Evaluation is the final ingredient in the Birth of a Family recipe.

OBJECTIVE
Experience Birth of a Family firsthand. Encounter the fruit. Tell the story. (John 15:16)

GET STARTED
The words "get started" have never been more appropriate in this recipe than right now. It's time to taste the fruit of your work using this recipe.

Birth of a Family isn't just research-based—it is evidence-based. This recipe is not based wholly on theoretical research. It is based on firsthand experience of more than three decades of well-studied, close-contact relational-discipleship. The evidence doesn't get more applicable than that.

It's time for you to experience your own evidence. To experience the evidence, you must have the experiences. In the following step-by-step suggestions, you will:

- ⊙ Create your Evaluation Survey

- ⊙ Experience a pilot series of at least twelve recurring Birth of a Family relational-discipleship activities

- ⊙ Evaluate your experiences

CREATE YOUR EVALUATION SURVEY

Your Evaluation Survey will validate your efforts, prove their effectiveness, encourage your team, and acknowledge God's graceful redemption.

TIPS

- ⊙ When developing your Plan, you've already set goals that should be included in your Evaluation Survey. Refer to your Plan while creating your Evaluation Survey.

- ⊙ Use the Evaluation Survey template in the template package you downloaded from the Birth of a Family website.

- ⊙ Your creativity and customization are encouraged as you develop your Evaluation Survey. Adapt the template to your satisfaction.

SUGGESTIONS

- ⊙ Go to the template package you downloaded from the Birth of a Family website.

- ⊙ From the template package, open the Evaluation Survey template in a spreadsheet application such as Microsoft Excel, Apple Numbers, or Google Sheets.

- ⊙ Notice that the Evaluation Survey template already includes three sections: Plan, Experience, and Adaptations.

- ⊙ In the first section, you will evaluate the Birth of a Family Plan you created earlier in this recipe.

- In the second section, you will evaluate your Birth of a Family experiences. Your first evaluation will be of your initial pilot series of Birth of a Family activities.

- In the third section, you will evaluate Adaptations that you may have already made or may want to consider for the future.

- Notice that the Evaluation Survey template is already formatted for Likert-scale responses.

- On the Likert scale in the Evaluation Survey template, 1 represents strong disagreement, and 5 represents strong agreement.

- A limited number of suggested statements are included in the Evaluation Survey template.

- Notice that the last column in the Evaluation Survey template is reserved for more-detailed comments.

- Review the Evaluation Survey template. Make the modifications that you feel suit your situation and the people being served best, and save your working copy.

- Use your Evaluation Survey regularly, beginning immediately after your initial pilot series of Birth of a Family relational-discipleship activities.

EXPERIENCE A PILOT SERIES

Ring the dinner bell, and let the fun begin. Now that you have an Evaluation Survey, it's time to experience a pilot series of at least twelve recurring Birth of a Family relational-discipleship activities. At least twelve consecutive Birth of a Family activities are needed to objectively evaluate your experiences.

Not only will you learn much from your first pilot series of Birth of a Family activities, but also transformational relationships will develop, people will connect in ways they never have, and root causes will be addressed.

> *"Ring the dinner bell, and let the fun begin."*

Evaluation

- Don't worry. A perfect Birth of a Family Plan isn't necessary. If you have followed this recipe reasonably well, your Birth of a Family Plan is sufficient.

- Because this experience will involve people and relationships, there will be surprises. That's normal.

- Birth of a Family experiences have a sticky quality. Once people have these experiences, they want to keep on having them. That's normal, and it's a sign of sustainability.

- As people engage in relational-discipleship during your pilot series of Birth of a Family, changes will begin to happen. Some changes will be difficult. That's normal.

- Numbers do not need to be high for your pilot to be successful. One, two, or three changed lives are far better than fifty well-entertained or merely enlightened people.

- Don't flinch. If you have followed this recipe, you have sought God and are responding to Him right now. Connecting fathers' hearts to their children and the Body of Christ to life-affirming ministry is an exceptionally ambitious challenge that is not as popular as it should be. It will require persistent work that must be carefully done.

- There are no easy ways to do this, but it will be rewarding.

SUGGESTIONS

- Use your Birth of a Family Plan.

- If you haven't already set dates, return to the Diligence ingredient in this recipe, and set dates for your first pilot series of Birth of a Family activities and your first Birth of a Family Informational Workshop.

- If you haven't already engaged the people you need, return to the Diligence ingredient in this recipe, and commission the work involved in your first pilot series of Birth of a Family activities.

◎ If you haven't already prepared for the changes Birth of a Family will generate, return to the Diligence ingredient in this recipe, and get ready to incorporate relational-discipleship as a key catalyst in your ministry model and strategy. Changes may include:

- Shifts in your ministry model or strategies
- New people involved in new ways
- New people served in new ways
- Deeper personal involvement in people's lives
- Unprecedented transformation
- New strategic engagement with other agencies

◎ During your Birth of a Family Informational Workshops, enlist, equip, and engage people of the Body of Christ to serve as your Birth of a Family Coordinators, Facilitators, and Mentors.

◎ Invite people to be Participants in your recurring Birth of a Family relational-discipleship activities.

◎ Optimize your Birth of a Family experiences to suit your situation and the people being served.

◎ Experience at least twelve recurring Birth of a Family relational-discipleship activities.

◎ Remain resolutely committed.

◎ Remember the five golden rules:

- Show up. In other words, be consistently present. Even if no Participants show up, continue your pilot series of Birth of a Family activities. If you build a sustainable Birth of a Family community, people will come.

- Be nice. In other words, ensure a welcoming, congenial atmosphere during your Birth of a Family activities.

- Show no condemnation. People involved in your Birth of a Family activities will be diverse. Ensure Christlike concern for all people.

Evaluation

- Speak truth in love. In other words, ensuring Christlike love for others is what opens doors for truth.

- Offer Biblically grounded role modeling, mentoring, and support. In other words, promote relational-discipleship that is consistent with God's word, not the ways of this world.

- Capture stories and key performance indicators.

EVALUATE YOUR EXPERIENCES

Within two weeks after completing your initial pilot series of Birth of a Family relational-discipleship activities, use your Evaluation Survey to prove the effectiveness of your Birth of a Family experiences.

TIPS

- Schedule your evaluation to occur within two weeks after completing your initial pilot series of Birth of a Family relational-discipleship activities.

- Compile and summarize key performance indicators prior to your evaluation.

SUGGESTIONS

- Set a date for your evaluation.

- Invite your Key Operatives to help you evaluate.

- Request RSVPs from people invited to help you evaluate.

- Consider asking your Birth of a Family Participants for input and testimonials.

- Use your Evaluation Survey to evaluate your Plan, Experiences, and Adaptations.

- Where possible, assign numeric and monetary values to your outputs, outcomes, and impacts.

- Write an executive summary of your evaluation findings.

ANTICIPATION

ANTICIPATION

"The Birth of a Famiy recipe ignites anticipation."

The Birth of a Family recipe is exuberant with hope for things unseen, for change unimaginable, and for children yet to be born. (Hebrews 11:1, Psalms 70:1-6)

This closing case study occurred at a time when all we could do was hope that Birth of a Family would work. At the time, our situation was much like yours might be right now. We had never actually experienced Birth of a Family firsthand, but we knew God wanted us to do so. Nothing like Birth of a Family had ever happened before. This book hadn't been written, and Birth of a Family's potential had not yet been proven. Still, we were excited about what God might do.

In 2006, after almost a year of research and development, we had a well-conceived plan for Birth of a Family and a great opportunity to put it to the test. The research basis for Birth of a Family was as solid as a rock. The plan was right out of the Bible, and the vote for creating our first, new Birth of a Family community was unanimous. But we still lacked the firsthand experience.

> *"Exuberant with hope for things unseen, for change unimaginable, and for children yet to be born."*

The very first series of pilot activities of Birth of a Family relational-discipleship activities began on a Tuesday night. Everyone there that night was taking a step into unknown territory. We knew very little about the Participants, and we were unsure how open they would be to building relationships with church people.

Larry and Sandy had been married for 50 years. They were trained to be Mentors. A couple from a local church with tough marriage issues agreed to give Birth of a Family a try. Phil and Barb were trained Mentors, and my wife, Vickie, and I were Facilitators.

John and Cindy arrived right on time that night with their newborn twins. Cindy was a client of the hosting pregnancy center. A short flurry of chaos erupted as they entered the room with their tandem stroller. We must have looked like aliens to John and Cindy. We were so different. This was the moment we had been anticipating for so long. Pregnancy-center clients and people of the Body were in the room to make transformational connections like never before.

It was awkward for everyone at first. About ten minutes into the activity, a subtle act of kindness changed everything. While the adults continued their awkward conversations, Phil, a Mentor in his sixties, began quietly talking with the newborn twins. The relational bonds were almost instant. The awkwardness melted away as if it had never been there. Within minutes, Cindy handed one of the twins to Phil, and the infant stayed in Phil's arms for the rest of the activity.

This momentous shift into relationships, trust, and rapport has since become a trademark quality of the Birth of a Family experience.

> "The relational bonds were almost instant."

Fast-forward three years. John and Cindy and their twins are still together. Their lifestyles have changed immensely. Phil and Barb have become like family to John, Cindy, and the twins. But God isn't done yet. He's only just begun.

By now, you have guessed this is a miraculous-turnaround story. In fact, it is. Several years after that first meeting, Phil and Barb were still connected to the family and were fondly viewed as mentors and adopted grandparents. Phil contacted us to relay a request from John and Cindy that they wanted to meet with Stuart to plan their marriage ceremony. When Stuart arrived at their home, John was not yet home from work, so he waited on the porch and visited with Cindy and her four-year-old twins. Sounds of an occasional car passing by on the gravel road could be heard while the twins were playing on the floor. Suddenly, from across the porch, the twins jumped up and ran toward the porch steps. They had learned to distinguish the sound of their father's car rolling down the gravel road. They couldn't wait to greet him. For the next hour, those children and their father were inseparable.

While John and Cindy explained their wedding wishes, it was hard to believe this was actually happening! Then, like a ton of bricks, it hit Stuart! John had been here supporting and parenting his family the whole time! Despite many difficulties, he had never left his family. After I left, the sight of the twins running into their father's arms kept playing over and over in his mind.

There are hundreds of stories like this today. We have come to expect them from Birth of a Family, and we are never let down. God iced the cake when He led John and Cindy to ask me to perform their covenant wedding in the front yard of their home almost four years after meeting them for the first time at a Birth of a Family relational-discipleship activity. The turnaround could not be more vivid.

> *"There are hundreds of stories like this today."*

Our hope for things unseen, for change unimaginable, and for the well-being of children yet to be born has shifted over the years. Two decades ago, we hoped to witness the transformational connection of fathers' hearts to their children and the Body of Christ to life-affirming ministry the way God wants them to be connected. Now, our hope is for *you* to experience Birth of a Family firsthand and encounter the fruit.

THE AUTHORS

That generations to come, even children yet to be born,
will know, trust and adore our Great God.
—Psalm 78

Before they were married, Stuart and Vickie made a deal that shaped their lives. In 1981, their relationships had grown and come to an awkward crossroads. They both wanted to build a family together, but they didn't want to do it the world's way. Their ultimatum to each other was, "God's way or no way." Without really knowing what they were doing, they literally shook hands in agreement to take the leap toward God's ways for their marriage and their family.

At that moment, they thought they were making an agreement with each other. As they later learned, God had more in mind. One thing led to another and their pursuit of family, God's way, began to draw others in. Within their first ten years of marriage, Stuart and Vickie were engaged in regular relational-discipleship activities where people were helping people turn toward God and His ways for their families. In 2004, they co-founded the Family God's Way movement, and, in 2006, their first relational-discipleship platform, *Birth of a Family*, was created.

They didn't know it at the time, but inside their handshake in 1981, a triune covenant was formed that included more than just the two of them. God had much more in mind. As their family and friends will tell you, God gave Stuart and Vickie an insatiable hunger to help people turn toward God and say, "Your way!"

Stuart is a pastor who is driven to engage the Body of Christ as the leading agent of change in the world, and Vickie is a Florida Licensed Mental Health Counselor and Gottman Bringing Baby Home

Educator. Together, Vickie and Stuart have worked to share Birth of a Family in the United States and globally. They have enjoyed more than 40 years of marriage, parenting, and, now, grand-parenting. At their rural home, gardening, beekeeping, and inventing new ways to build lasting memories with their family are favorite pastimes. They also love to cook.

Printed in the USA
CPSIA information can be obtained
at www.ICGtesting.com
LVHW060523140124
768571LV00002B/2